RECRUITING STRATEGIES FOR PUBLIC SCHOOLS

Herbert F. Pandiscio

Published in partnership with the
American Association of School Administrators

Rowman & Littlefield Education
Lanham, Maryland • Toronto • Oxford
2005

Published in partnership with
the American Association of School Administrators

Published in the United States of America
by Rowman & Littlefield Education
A Division of Rowman & Littlefield Publishers, Inc.
A wholly owned subsidary of The Rowman & Littlefield Publishing Group, Inc.
4501 Forbes Boulevard, Suite 200, Lanham, Maryland 20706
www.rowmaneducation.com

PO Box 317
Oxford
OX2 9RU, UK

British Library Cataloguing in Publication Information Available

Library of Congress Cataloging-in-Publication Data
Pandiscio, Herbert F. (Herbert Frederick), 1931–
   Recruiting strategies for public schools / Herbert F. Pandiscio.
   p. cm.
   "Published in partnership with the American Association of School
Administrators."
   Includes bibliographical references and index.
   ISBN 1-57886-233-7 (pbk. : alk. paper)
   1. Teachers—Recruiting—United States. 2. Affirmative action programs
in education—United States. 3. Teachers—Selection and appointment—
United States. I. Title.

LB2835.25.P36 2005
331.7'6113711'00973—dc22   2004024859

∞™ The paper used in this publication meets the minimum requirements of
American National Standard for Information Sciences—Permanence of Paper
for Printed Library Materials, ANSI/NISO Z39.48-1992.
Manufactured in the United States of America.

To Curt, Eric, and Margaret

CONTENTS

ON MY HONOR, I PROMISE . . .

On my honor, I promise with the moral and legal authority I possess to provide each candidate who applies for a position in my school system an equal opportunity to compete for and to be appointed to a position for which he or she is qualified in keeping with the Board of Education Policy No. 6140, "Equal Opportunity in Hiring." Further, I will take whatever steps are necessary to implement said policy. All positions will be advertised in appropriate media and posted in keeping with applicable law and employee contracts, and a reasonable period will be provided in order that prospective candidates can learn of and apply for open positions. I guarantee that all positions will be filled with the most qualified candidates after a rigorous examination of credentials and experiences.

On my honor, I will oppose hiring that is driven by patronage whether generated internally or externally, and that the administration will develop and implement a process by which all applications for positions will be processed in an equitable manner; that the recruiting process will be documented for all to witness; that written assessments or narratives will be created for each and every candidate; that such documents will be open for viewing by those who have an interest in and a right to view under the applicable law; that all evaluations of candidates will be in written form, signed by the evaluator(s).

On my honor, I guarantee that all employees who participate in the recruiting process will be educated in appropriate protocols, governing board policies, and employee contracts and that they will abide by all state and national mandates and local ordinances; further, any deviation from the process will be reported to the superintendent who in turn will inform the governing board in open session of any such deviations.

On my honor, I promise to place children in the custody and care of only those who are qualified, who are appointed to their positions by virtue of a fair and open competition, and who are judged as qualified by those capable of making such judgments.

On my honor, all who apply for positions in this district and all who are currently employed in the Doering Public Schools will be informed in writing of this pledge.

Signed: Tony Wilson, Superintendent of Schools
Dated: January 1, 2005

WHO CAN PROFIT FROM THIS GUIDE?

This guide is designed for many audiences but primarily for superintendents (and those who represent them in the recruiting process) and governing boards and their members. It is a companion to my first guide, *Job Hunting in Education*, which was written for those seeking positions in education. This guide is written for those who actually do the hiring.

Job Hunting in Education, although written for candidates seeking employment, made frequent reference to those responsible for hiring and the responsibility they have to ensure that a district's hiring protocols are, without exception, fair to all candidates. Based on my experiences with over a hundred governing boards and with those responsible for hiring employees, it is evident that each district involved in the recruiting process falls somewhere on a continuum of excellent, average, poor, and unacceptable when it comes to the quality of equitable service given to recruiting. Some districts are outstanding in the hiring process, most are adequate, and others are shamefully lacking in professionalism. An "adequate" performance is, in my mind, an inadequate performance when one weighs the negative impact that a flawed recruiting system has on those candidates who were eliminated from consideration because of the failures of a recruiting process or system.

While recruiting is within the province of a human relations department in large districts, it is often assigned to an assistant superintendent in medium-sized districts. In small districts, it usually is the responsibility of the superintendent. Nevertheless, regardless of who has the operational responsibility for the recruiting program, the governing board establishes policy, and the superintendent is responsible for its implementation.

Governing boards and individual members of governing boards must be ever vigilant that the recruiting process in their districts is firmly grounded on ethical and moral footings. They must assure the public and all candidates applying for positions that those in leadership positions never veer from established hiring protocols. Collectively and individually, governing board members must refrain from any actions or comments that could be construed as applying pressure on those accountable for the hiring process.

Superintendents cannot retreat from their responsibility to implement the policy of the governing board. Responsible for the oversight of the recruiting program, they can never abandon the ethical and moral basis upon which recruitment is based. No aspect of a district's efforts to improve education is more vital than the recruitment of teachers and administrators. Throughout this guide, emphasis is placed on the importance that recruiting has in a district's effort to promote the interests of students. The integrity of a school system will be measured in large part by the quality of its recruiting system and the roles that superintendents and governing boards play in creating a level playing field.

In addition to the primary audiences (governing boards and superintendents) for this guide, there are others who will profit from it. They include the following:

1. Human relations department personnel, who have the responsibility to implement the ethical and moral principles that the board has established and that the superintendent must support.
2. Assistant superintendents and other central office personnel, who often act in lieu of a human relations department and who have the responsibility to be fair to all candidates as they lead the recruiting effort.

3. Building-level administrators, who often are among the first to identify, from among the many applicants, those who will be selected to move forward in the process. They are in a position to either honor or distort the process in its initial phase.

4. Teachers and administrators who serve on screening or interviewing committees, for they must exert caution not to give unfair advantage to long-serving substitutes or paraprofessionals in their schools or to those who are friends, parents, and neighbors.

5. Teachers and administrators applying for new positions who, through the information in this guide, will be better able to discern if they are applicants navigating in a district with a fair recruiting process.

6. Undergraduate and graduate education majors who, after studying how recruiters go about their task of hiring, will know the questions to ask about the recruiting process and be able to detect if it is being played out on a level field with a spirit of fairness.

7. College and university educators who prepare students to enter the job market, for they have the responsibility to equip students for the many recruiting journeys that lie ahead.

8. Those in private industry who may be considering a career move to a job in education.

9. Every person who is considering a position in public school education, for it is to his or her advantage to understand how the public sector recruiting process works.

CREDIT

Throughout this book, reference is made to the author's first book, *Job Hunting in Education*. Rowman & Littlefield Education (formerly Scare-crowEducation), 4501 Forbes Boulevard, Suite 200, Lanham, MD 20706, publishes *Job Hunting in Education*. The book has a copyright date of 2004 and was first published in April 2004. *Job Hunting in Education* may be ordered online at www.rowmaneducation.com.

GLOSSARY/TERMINOLOGY

This guide addresses the hiring process and those who are responsible for developing, implementing, and monitoring the program. Recruiting takes place at many levels in a typical school system, and it is designed to hire employees in many job categories. This guide addresses the hiring of what is often referred to as *professional staff members*, who require state certification, in contrast to those in noncertified positions, such as secretaries, clerks, and custodial workers.

The professional, certified staff generally includes classroom teachers, support teachers, pupil personnel staff (such as counselors and social workers), department chairpersons, central office administrators, building principals, and superintendents. There will be other job categories depending on the size and configuration of a school system.

Because of the range of positions to be filled and the many titles ascribed to those who do the selecting, this guide shifts back and forth among many titles as it describes the recruiting process. Consequently, those responsible for hiring may be referred to as *recruiter, hiring agent, superintendent, governing board, human relations personnel,* and other titles. All of the individuals who possess these titles have one thing in common; namely, in whatever context a title is used, it refers to the person responsible for the hiring process in that situation.

We should remember that the governing board sets the recruiting policy and that the superintendent implements and monitors it, as well as establishes the ethical and moral guidelines for the staff.

ACKNOWLEDGMENTS

Thanks to Ruth Pandiscio, friend, search firm partner, critic/editor, and wife whose belief in, support of, and help with this manuscript was unwavering.

Thanks also to Russell F. Farnen, of Farmington, Connecticut, professor of political science and former director of the University of Connecticut, Hartford Regional Campus in West Hartford, who gave so generously of his time to edit this guide and who provided ideas for reorganization of the materials.

INTRODUCTION

This book is about recruiting teachers for public schools and is a guide for all who, in one way or another, participate in the hiring process. My opinions reflect my thirty-five years of recruiting in the public sector. During that period, I experienced a variety of recruiting practices, from outstanding to inadequate.

The book is both a guideline for action and a caution to those who have failed or who may fail to create a level recruiting field for candidates. This is a book about honor, about a promise to respect all candidates regardless of race, color, gender, religion, or other persuasions. It is about strength—the strength of superintendents and governing boards to withstand the pressures of patronage, favoritism, and other unethical influences from without and within the system.

A word about myself and the organization of the book is appropriate. Chapters 1 through 20 address specific topics that will be of interest and assistance to all recruiters and their colleagues. All of the data presented are based on my personal experiences as a recruiter. Chapter 21, "How Did Underperformers Come to Be Hired?" identifies methods that can be employed to identify underperforming teachers, typical of the thousands of teachers across the nation who, because of an inadequate recruiting system and unqualified recruiters, are employed to staff our classrooms and who now fail to educate our children. The identification of these underperformers sets the stage for the final chapter.

Chapter 22, "The Vetting Process: Anecdotes and Lessons Learned," identifies the recruiting failures that lead to the hiring of underperformers, failures that serve as valuable lessons for all recruiters. The chapter comprises twenty-three anecdotes and twenty-three valuable recruiting lessons for superintendents, governing boards, and those to whom the recruiting responsibility has been delegated. The anecdotes are those that most superintendents and governing board members will easily recognize.

I began my career as a teacher in one of the nation's "lighthouse" school systems. It was a district that taught many lessons about creativity in teaching, including curriculum exploration, program design and experimentation, student-grouping practices, and modular scheduling—lessons that have guided me throughout my career. But of far greater importance, it was a district that mastered the art of recruiting, the primary foundation on which notable United States school districts are built.

This book is about my experiences in that lighthouse district, as a teacher and as a department head; it is also about my extensive experiences in several other districts where I implemented many of the ideas developed while in the lighthouse district. The book is also about thirty-five years of recruiting experience, both as a superintendent and as a search consultant.

Finally, a word is necessary as it relates to the lighthouse district in which I began my career and where I acquired my philosophical underpinning for recruiting, which remained with me throughout my career. It is a district similar to a limited number of others that wanted more for its students than was typically provided in the majority of school districts at that time.

The story begins with the period before World War II, when there were relatively few suburbs as we know them today. Those that existed were mostly upper- and upper-middle-class private preserves. Both groups comprised mostly successful entrepreneurs and business executives. They worked in the central cities, where their businesses were located, and they commuted to their suburban enclaves, where they lived comfortably. There, they were immune from the pedestrian values of the relatively uneducated middle- and lower-class citizens. They were better educated and enjoyed the luxuries that wealth afforded them. While the privileged enjoyed the benefits of the suburbs, the majority of other citizens lived in cities and rural areas and worked in the nation's factories and farms.

It was not until after World War II that the nation experienced an explosion in the number of suburban districts and the distribution of wealth.

Eager to regain some semblance of normality, returning veterans married, had families, and were soon in need of housing. Because the housing stock in the cities was limited and not always desirable, returning veterans flocked to newly developing suburbs. At the same time, the GI Bill provided unprecedented educational opportunities for discharged veterans. One wonders if the architects of that legislation envisioned the dramatic impact it would have on the nation. In just a short period, the nation experienced a quantum leap in the number of educated citizens, people who wanted their children to have even better educational opportunities than they had. Thus was born the modern educational movement in terms of putting into practice the ideal that all children had a right to a free, full, extended public education. Veterans of the war who earned a college degree or received vocational training directly experienced the economic value of public education.

While the federal government provided veterans with free and generous educational opportunities, cooperative federalism also pumped billions of dollars into educational initiatives. Russian technological advances, symbolized by Sputnik, spurred Americans to action. While the "hot" war was over, the "cold" war had begun in earnest. This contest was in large measure responsible for the emphasis our government placed on providing a quality education for our citizens. Education was accepted as the salvation of our democracy.

From the days of our founding fathers, education was viewed as a way to secure the future of the nation and protect it from the expansionary goals of other powers. Our victorious records in World Wars I and II provided strong evidence of the value of talented workers who could produce new weapons to arm the professional and volunteer citizen soldiers and guarantee our national security.

Colleges and universities were employed to channel government funding into elementary and secondary education. It was the influx of government funds that provided for educational experimentation, new teaching strategies, and the development of advanced curriculum materials. The government placed special emphasis on improvement in the teaching of science, mathematics, and foreign languages. The district in which I worked as a teacher was the recipient of vast amounts of government funds. These funds were dedicated to the development of new curriculum ideas—ideas that ultimately placed enormous pressure on the district to recruit outstanding teachers, especially in the fields of science, mathematics, and foreign languages. This is a stimulative aspect of the post-1957 curriculum revolution that is often ignored.

It was during the exciting period of the 1950s and 1960s, in particular, that public education saw the development of lighthouse schools and school districts. What was it about these districts that set them aside from thousands of other districts? What made them so special? Why did students in these districts achieve at high levels while millions of other students did not succeed? Were the educational leaders, teachers, and administrators better trained or educated? Did the massive infusion of government funding make the difference, or were funds diverted to these districts because they were so outstanding? What impact did the visions of governing boards play in the development of these districts? Did better-educated parents provide the driving force for change? Did Russia's threat of dominance and its harnessing nuclear weapons and developing intercontinental missiles motivate schools to improve? Or was it the result of a shift in the socioeconomic structure wherein better-educated parents saw evidence that middle- and upper-class suburban schools outscored their lower-class urban and rural counterparts? The answer, of course, is "all of the above."

Yet, there were two primary initiatives that drove school improvement during this era. First, the superintendent was usually at the head of the vanguard of change and improvement in lighthouse districts. Without visionaries at the head of the line, there is no parade! Second, governing boards in these districts demonstrated courage to support change, for no superintendent has even a remote chance to succeed in developing an outstanding school system without such support.

Having worked in a lighthouse school system at the outset of my career, and then having taken the ideas on which this school system was founded to other systems, I have identified five basic initiatives on which a successful school system is usually built.

The first focuses on professional staff development for every new employee. Whether new or experienced, employees come to an outstanding district only partly prepared to meet the demands of the position.

The second initiative is a comprehensive curriculum renewal cycle that guarantees student achievement and effective teaching.

The third is a comprehensive employee evaluation program that guarantees that only the most competent remain and advance in the district.

The fourth is a comprehensive student-testing program that validates the work of the classroom teacher and building administrator.

The fifth, and most important, without which none of the other four can be fully realized, is a well-structured, ethically based recruiting program that eliminates patronage, creates a level playing field for all candidates, and discourages administrators from playing favorites with candidates from within and outside the district. The cold, hard truth is that, absent highly qualified personnel, a district's professional development program will have no competent in-house trainers; curriculum renewal will be unattainable; the employee evaluation plan will lack talented supervisors and evaluators; and the district's student testing program will produce mixed or unsatisfactory results. Whatever money is spent on education, most will be squandered if classrooms are not staffed with outstanding teachers and if qualified administrators do not run buildings!

It is the fifth and last initiative, the development of an outstanding recruiting program, that is the focus of this book. In my very first teaching position, I recognized the necessity for an effective recruiting program in the lighthouse district, as well as in many of the districts in which I subsequently worked for thirty years serving as chief school administrator and search consultant.

When a district hires effectively, it saves an immense amount of time, energy, and money in not having to recycle employees who do not possess the capacity to meet high district standards. It eliminates placing the superintendent, staff, and the governing board under the enormous pressure and stress that results from efforts to terminate unqualified and underperforming teachers and administrators. It makes unnecessary the expenditure of funds for legal counsel. When a district hires the very best, it is in a win-win situation.

Throughout this book, the case is made that the superintendent is singularly accountable for the recruiting program, regardless of who has been delegated the responsibility. The superintendent alone gives assurance to the community that only the most competent teachers and administrators staff district schools. Once a district offers a contract of employment, it has a damnable time later trying to unload an unsatisfactory employee, whether tenured or not.

One can only wonder how many school superintendents would be willing to put a signature to a pledge like the one at the beginning of this book, which begins, "On my honor, I promise . . ."

❶

I GUARANTEE

Upon arrival in a school system, the superintendent needs to take charge of the hiring process. The recruiting process is the single most effective way for a superintendent to set the tone and direction for a school system, particularly a system seeking improvement and change. Unfortunately, most superintendents do not remain in their positions long enough to dramatically affect the quality of the staff. Those that do remain often fail to understand the importance of setting the standard for recruiting. Too often it is delegated it to others, some of whom have never been in a classroom or managed a building. Consequently, because of a marginal recruiting system, superintendents often make demands of those who are simply not up to the task. Teachers hired without talent do not achieve it by osmosis. It is no surprise, therefore, that many school districts fail to help their students. One can only ponder the incredible damage inflicted daily on hundreds of thousands of unsuspecting students!

Superintendents who remain in their positions for any length of time should understand that the recruiting cycle begins with a statement of principle, whether the statement is a policy or a set of written protocols. In either case, superintendents need to initiate the process.

The development of a written protocol is essential to the initiation of an effective hiring program. Without a vision for recruiting, a district travels from one crisis to another. For districts that need additional comfort, a recruiting protocol can easily be designed as a governing board policy. Whatever the format, the protocol provides substantial protection to superintendents and their staffs as they honor every candidate and work tirelessly to maintain a level playing field. A superintendent who is unwilling or unable to guarantee that every candidate has equal access to an open or new position should relinquish his or her own position.

There is no other task performed by a superintendent that requires such strict adherence to state and federal statutes and negotiated contracts with employees as does recruiting. Failure to ensure equity in hiring is inexcusable for a school superintendent. For the leader, there is no retreating from protecting the rights of others. There is an implicit responsibility to defend fair employment practices. Adherence to state and federal statutes does not necessarily mean that fair employment practices are guaranteed. For example, poorly trained interviewing committee members may be reluctant to ask a minority candidate if he or she will be able to contend with potential social isolation if he or she were the only minority teacher in a school building with no apparent community support system. It is an important question to ask and a fair one. If the question is not asked, some members of the interviewing committee may believe that social isolation will occur and that the candidate's teaching would be negatively affected. That is an unfair assumption and would give an edge to a white candidate, who would not face this challenge in a white community. Only the minority candidate can answer the question with authority. This example, reversed, would be a disservice to a white candidate applying for a position in a predominately minority community.

The most profound way to protect the rights of candidates is for a superintendent to vigorously support three basic guarantees. The fact that they may not be a written part of the formal recruiting program is irrelevant: they are moral and ethical mandates that must be shouldered by the leader. It is for the superintendent to state unequivocally that "I guarantee . . ."

THE FIRST BASIC GUARANTEE

A recruiting protocol must have an underlying belief that all new hires must and will be appropriately inducted into the school system. The induction implies a formal, ongoing, professional, and appropriate orientation program. It also assumes that only a small percentage of new hires will meet all of a district's professional criteria at the time of hiring. A district never achieves perfection in a hiring program, although perfection must remain its goal. Perfection is achieved only after a recruiter has contracted with the most outstanding teachers and administrators available at the time of hiring and has inducted them into the school system through a formal training program. The program also takes experienced but often professionally immature educators through a professional development program and provides appropriate training. A district makes a serious misjudgment if it assumes that years of experience are equivalent to professional maturity. Too often, this is the case. It is important to keep in mind that a twenty-year veteran may have had the same experiences twenty times over! We all have heard of teachers who work from the same lesson plans year after year regardless of what the formal curriculum may be. There are building principals who cherish the past at the expense of innovation and improvement. For many, staying out of trouble is the annual goal.

A written protocol must make it readily apparent to whoever is making the final hiring decision that all potential new employees must be judged in part on their willingness to participate in professional development, regardless of experience level. Moreover, the superintendent must personally guarantee all new hires that the professional development program, whatever its format, will justify their joining the system.

THE SECOND BASIC GUARANTEE

The superintendent must be a hero, an educator who champions contract language with the local teacher and administrator representative groups that provides for two critical contract terms. The contract must have a highly competitive salary schedule for all employees but in particular for entry-level teachers and administrators. When there is a surplus of candidates, this provision is less important than when there is an acute staff shortage. So often, the most experienced teachers are on the negotiating team and tend to "take care of those at the top."

When I was a teenager, my mom and dad ran a department store. I spent all of my spare time in the store and learned early in life the meaning of customer service, although it was not called as such in those days. The business mantra was "The customer is always right." I can recall vividly my mom constantly reminding my father that the inventory was too large and therefore too costly to carry. My dad's response was always the same: "You can't sell from an empty wagon." If a district does not have "a full wagon," in this case salary and benefits to offer to candidates, it is "selling from an empty wagon," which will significantly reduce the chances of attracting the most qualified educators to your district.

Occasionally, a district will get lucky and employ someone who needs a job at that particular moment, or someone whose spouse is transferred and so the move requires a candidate to take the first position offered, or someone just plain desperate for work and willing to take the compensation offered. However, it would be professional suicide for a district to depend on luck to staff its schools.

Superintendents must also fight for a contract provision that allows them to hire at any step on the teacher and administrator salary schedule without first receiving the permission of the teacher's or the administrator's association. This flexibility provides a great opportunity to hire the most outstanding candidates. Hand in hand with this contract condition, the superintendents must have the ability to convince the governing board that they must not be restricted to where on the salary grid a new teacher or administrator may be placed. To be competitive in the marketplace, you must be able to use placement on the salary grid as a recruiting weapon. Superintendents cannot use as an excuse the fact that a governing board or a board's attorney negotiates the contract and that they have no role in its development. Superintendents are paid to be aggressive in promoting what is best for their school systems. A superintendent must be able to hire teachers and administrators without the approval of the governing board.

THE THIRD BASIC GUARANTEE

The hiring process must have an impenetrable firewall that separates it from the patronage system. This is easier said than done, but a superintendent must have the courage to confront the patronage issue without hesitation. When patronage is mentioned, one might logically assume that it describes the political pressure that is applied to the human relations personnel, the superintendent, and the governing board members when friends, relatives, and political cronies of powerful politicians apply for employment. This pressure comes from outside the school system. Indeed, it is a powerful force, sometimes overwhelming. It is the most common type of pressure and is often visible to others. It is covered in detail in chapter 3, "If You Can't Stand the Pressure . . ."

There is a second form of inside patronage, one not often visible from the outside but one that must be confronted. While there are no official data available, it is a well-known fact that a high percentage of administrators are married to other educators. It logically follows that spouses and other family members of superintendents will be employed by superintendents in other districts. In these instances some percentage of superintendents will come perilously close to penetrating the patronage firewall. In some instances they will in fact penetrate it. Superintendents need to keep flawless, potentially public records of the interviewing process, particularly the written assessments of candidates that were completed at all stages of the process. They also need to be explicit in their directions to employees that everyone engaged in the hiring process will make no exceptions to the written protocols. A superintendent must be able to justify to an objective third party, such as local radio, television, and newspapers, that the hiring of friends, relatives, and others who may be related to other superintendents or other influential educators was within the parameters of the recruiting guide or policy. Any exceptions can lead to the undoing of a superintendent. In conducting background checks on superintendents who have applied for positions for which my firm was recruiting, I discovered that a number of them were nonrenewed because they inappropriately hired friends, relatives, and, in one case, a lover.

The media have proven to be unrelenting in pursuing alleged wrong-doing, especially involving high-level officials. Such public exposure could seriously compromise school administrators, whom the public wants to view as positive role models. Even though school administrators may believe that they have won a media battle, they may well have lost it in the minds of the general public. Worse still, the resulting discredit has a way of clinging to public officials forever.

Yielding to patronage is an ugly event unbecoming to all public officials, especially superintendents who are entrusted with the lives of children. It is inappropriate behavior for those on the inside—for example, school superintendents—to bemoan outside pressure that may be applied to them in the recruiting process while using the system to their personal advantage. Either form of patronage is debilitating to a school system because it sends a message that the playing field is not level.

Large urban systems that have a powerful-mayor form of government are most susceptible to the patronage game because of the enormous influence the political structure has on school funding. To ignore this pressure takes a superintendent of considerable strength and character. Superintendents employed in rural areas and small suburbs are also subject to outside pressures. Often, one or two families run the town or have considerable influence over town politics. They are as skillful at applying pressure as are big city politicians! Superintendents in these districts face pressures not unlike those of their urban counterparts. Newer, emerging, pluralistic suburbs are less likely to feel these same intense pressures since many of those in political positions are new to the community and have little long-term influence.

As a superintendent of many years, I attempted to develop a system based on honor that, among other factors, addressed the question of patronage. If I could relive my career as a superintendent, I would strengthen my approach, requiring all employees who work on the recruiting program, particularly administrators, to maintain a written log of all conversations that are outside of the normal internal communications process. They would be required to maintain a record of all calls and visits from any person who attempted to promote a candidate outside of the established guidelines. This would protect them from accusations of favoritism and send a powerful message to those who would otherwise attempt to apply pressure.

The three basic guarantees may not be written into the recruiting protocols, but they are the silent conscience of a quality recruiting program. The superintendent must safeguard them at all times! Leadership is measured in large part by how vigorously one defends what is clearly right.

With the guarantees in place, chapter 2 begins the recruiting journey, ideally with a skillful driver at the wheel and an accurate map in hand.

②

WANTED: A SKILLFUL DRIVER
WITH AN ACCURATE MAP

The recruiting system is propelled by the superintendent, not the human relations department, for there is no single activity performed in a school system that influences the teaching and learning functions more than the quality of those who are employed to teach. What students are taught, how they are taught, and what they achieve are functions of the quality of the staff. It is a simple equation: a poorly qualified staff will teach poorly; a highly qualified staff will improve the academic lives of students.

If a superintendent were restricted to performing only one task, it would be, in my opinion, the complete management of the hiring process. This process requires skillful hands at the wheel. It is a process that speaks volumes about the integrity of the school system and the superintendent who leads it. The recruiting journey is not a function that one places in the hands of an inexperienced student driver!

While human relations personnel may draft the operational rules by which recruiting is conducted, only the superintendent has the authority to approve them. While others monitor adherence to rules, the superintendent has the responsibility to enforce them. While many others in the district implement the adopted rules, the superintendent is charged with safeguarding them. While some in the system attempt to skirt the rules, the superintendent guarantees adherence to them. When lesser-ranking administrators have pressure applied to them, the superintendent intervenes.

The hiring process is a complicated process, easily compromised if safeguards are not firmly in place. The slightest departure from agreed-upon protocols is a breach of trust.

When a candidate submits an application to a school district, there is an underlying assumption that it will be processed according to a strict set of rules, rules from which there can be no departure. There is an expectation by the candidate that fair employment practices are in place regardless of the size or complexity of the district. A candidate has the right to believe that his or her application has begun a journey through honorable hands.

There cannot be the slightest fissure in the recruiting system, allowing one candidate an unfair advantage over another. While a well-defined recruiting process exists primarily to allow a district to meet its employment needs, it also exists for the benefit of candidates who expend much time and energy to complete applications and compete in the process.

The only accurate method of guaranteeing that a recruiting system is evenhanded and candidate-friendly is for every district to develop written guidelines for each employee who in any way is involved in the hiring process. Anyone who has a role in processing an application or who speaks with a candidate needs guidance. The guidelines must include procedures for employees in every job category. Specific language must define what a governing board's role is in the process, and it must be especially specific to the limitations placed on individual board members when outside a formal sitting of the board. No employee or member of a governing board should be in a position where he or she can unduly interfere with the normal journey of an application through the process or influence a hiring decision. Even an administrative mishandling of an application is a serious matter.

Recruiting protocols are the equivalent of a roadmap. They allow the hiring agent to move from point A to point B and beyond until the process of employing a candidate is completed. Equally important as completing the journey is the fact that the protocols provide clear instructions about how to proceed from point A to point B. Written protocols also serve as contingency plans. Protocols are professional life preservers for employees who are being requested or pressured to veer from the established recruiting procedure. Just as the superintendent is the driver, the protocol is the roadmap that guarantees candidates equal access to jobs and protects employees who engage in fair play.

Most school systems in the nation have governing board policies and administrative regulations that address student behavior, teacher accountability, curricular cycles, testing programs, and dozens of other functions. These written protocols exist to spare teachers and administrators the grief that could result from their decisions. Effective protocols have language that is precise; the chain of command is clear, the process is clean, protection is provided for those who make ethical decisions, and there is an appeal process. A district that fails to put into place similar protocols for its hiring process does an injustice to anyone engaged in the effort. Superintendents who fail to provide leadership in developing a recruiting system with professional protocols can do irreparable damage to the school system and undermine the ethical foundation of the recruiting process.

Chapter 3 describes the dangerous pressures that may be applied to the recruiting process and the suggestions for sidestepping them.

③

IF YOU CAN'T STAND
THE PRESSURE . . .

PRESSURE FROM ON HIGH

One of the pressures inevitably exerted on a recruiting process origi-
nates from a member of the school district's governing body or from
members of other powerful boards in town. Chapter 2 made note of the
fact that language needs to be included in the recruiting guidelines that
clearly defines the governing board's role in the process and that speci-
fies the limitations placed on individual board members outside of their
formal membership on the board. It is vital that no employee or member of a governing board be in a position where he or she can interfere
with an application's normal flow through the process or influence a hiring decision.

Pressure on the process may run the gambit from subtle to direct.
Subtlety usually comes in the form of a comment from a board member,
such as "Tell me, did Tom McDonald apply for that opening in the social studies department at the middle school? I have heard he is a ter-
rific candidate. It would be great if my kids could have him in the fall.
You'd certainly make my family happy."

A not-so-subtle effort would be the following comment from a board
member: "Tony, I hear that Jake Wilkinson, chair of the Board of Finance,

has a son who applied for the assistant principal position at the high school. I know you appreciate how influential Jake is when it comes time to assess the Board of Education budget. He also has a good deal to say about your salary, and he has never approved of the substantial perks we give you."

Directly applied pressure is just that: "Tony, the mayor has made it clear that he wants his daughter to get that third-grade job at Louisville School. I know you will make it happen."

Pressure may come from the chair or from individuals on the board with or without the knowledge of the chair. Pressure can come from members of other town boards, politicians, and influential individuals in the community. Pressure may be applied at any point in the process, from the superintendent down to the lowest-ranking administrator; basically, it can be applied to anyone who has sufficient influence to move an application forward by skirting the formal process. It may come from members of the superintendent's staff who want a particular internal candidate "because I want her."

Pressure may be directed at the administrator in charge of the human relations department, who is often viewed as the one person who can manipulate the process before an application begins its journey. From wherever the pressure comes and from whomever it was initiated, the person so targeted must immediately report it to the superintendent. If the pressure is applied to the superintendent, he or she must bring it to the attention of the chair. If the pressure comes from the chair, the superintendent must, the first time it occurs, make it clear to the chair that all matters related to hiring are handled through the formal process. If it occurs a second time, the superintendent must bring it to the attention of the full board.

Although an individual governing board member has no authority outside of his or her formal sitting on the board, many individual members do not understand this fact or choose to ignore it. Given the extensive training available to board members through their professional organizations and relevant publications, it is difficult to believe that they are ignorant of the appropriate process. Thus, it is fair to conclude that most of them choose to ignore the information. It would be difficult to find a superintendent who has not had a member of his or her governing board imply, suggest, or even direct that a certain person be employed.

IF YOU CAN'T STAND THE PRESSURE . . .   I 5

THREE EXAMPLES OF APPLIED PRESSURE

Situation Number I: Low Pressure

In this first instance, I was approached by a member of a town board who represented "a friend" seeking a teaching position in one of my schools. This person who approached me was a member of a board that was influential in terms of assisting the superintendent and the board of education in meeting its educational mandates. While the approach was a subtle one, it was obvious that the board member wanted me to consider appointing his friend to a position. In this instance, I politely informed the board member that there was a formal process in place and that I would be pleased to meet with his friend to explain it. I also stated that the friend's application would have to be processed according to the official guidelines. That direct but polite response was accepted, and I never sensed any fallout from my decision. To this day, I have contact with this person, and we always extend professional courtesies to each other. This person no longer is a member of that board.

Situation Number 2: Serious Pressure

The second case was more serious in that a member of my own board quizzed me at a public session to why an applicant of a certain religious denomination was not hired. Although the specific religion was never mentioned, there was ample evidence about what faith was involved. At no time was I approached in private by the board member with this question. The board member was of the same denomination as the person not hired. The candidate had gone directly to the board member with her complaint, never having contacted me. The applicant had gone through the formal process, which included several interviews with written assessments completed after each interview. She was not selected because the interviewers did not view her as being as qualified as other candidates. She was not one of the three finalists for the position. If she had been, I would have interviewed her, along with others, since the practice was for the superintendent to interview the strongest three or four candidates as recommended by the building principal or screening committee. She was assessed as not being as qualified as other candidates.

The manner in which she responded to her not being hired led the administrator in charge to believe that there most likely would be some adverse fallout. He alerted me to this fact and briefed me on the details. In this case, I was forewarned and thus forearmed. However, a public board meeting was the last place I expected this matter to surface!

I paraphrase the question that the board member posed: "Herb, is the district prejudiced against certain religious faiths in its hiring policy?" Is it possible for a board member to be any more direct than that? Fortunately, an alert administrator forewarned me, but as mentioned, I had not anticipated that the matter would surface at a regular board meeting. Thankfully, at that stage in my career, I was sufficiently perceptive to know that I did not want to get into a religious faith debate. I also knew that the manner in which I responded was important. I would tackle this query straightforwardly, knowing that there was no cause for other board members to question my integrity or that of my staff who had made the recommendation not to hire. As far as I was concerned, this board member was alone in his thinking and would not be particularly influential. Nevertheless, the issue had the potential to escalate to a more serious level. I decided not to be defensive.

As is the case whenever I speak at a public session, I moved closer to the table, placed both my arms on it, looked directly at that one board member, never taking my eyes off him, and in a quiet voice spoke. "We hire in accordance with the written guidelines we have in place, which include a written assessment of all candidates. If a candidate is not hired, it is because a jury of peers and the administrator in charge viewed the candidate as not being as well qualified as other candidates and not able to meet the teaching standards of the district. This is a position that this and previous boards have long supported. We make no exceptions to these guidelines."

The board member nodded, spoke not a word, and the chair moved on to other agenda items. The most compelling reasons for the board member to drop this matter were the fact that I had a history of being fair, peers were involved in the decision, and the process was in accordance with written protocols. Without the protective elements of a protocol, the process would have been vulnerable. A less-experienced superintendent could easily have included a comment such as "We make no distinctions to religion." I chose not to introduce the word *religion* in my response.

Situation Number 3: Threatening Pressure

The third case was the most serious and led to an influential and politically powerful member of the community working to unseat me as superintendent. This person was looking to have a relative hired. As was the case in the example just given, a jury of peers did not view this person's relative as being qualified to teach in our district. The rejected candidate did not approach a board member; rather, she complained to her relative, who then complained to one of my key administrators with whom he was friendly, who then came to me with the matter. The decision not to hire the candidate was made by the professional staff. I chose not to second-guess my teachers and administrators. More important, I supported their professional decision.

Since the candidate did not complain to me, I remained silent. Some weeks later at another meeting in town, the relative asked why I did not hire the teacher in question. I explained the process, but it was clear that this was not to his satisfaction. He gave me what could only be described as a hostile look and with a shrug of his shoulders walked off in a huff. I knew that this behavior signaled the beginning of what turned out to be a difficult relationship, which continued for fifteen years. He worked behind the scenes to have me ousted as superintendent by using this and other incidents that occurred in the normal course of my work as a public official.

I could have ended the pressure on me by sidestepping the process and hiring his relative, but I would not and did not. Would I do the same now? Yes, because as mentioned in chapter 2, superintendents who fail to provide the leadership in developing a recruiting system with protocols and who fail to take a strong stand against patronage do irreparable damage to the school system and damage the ethical foundation of the recruiting process.

COINCIDENCE OR TALENT

A final word on what one might view as subtle pressure. During the years I worked as a consultant, I assumed interim superintendent positions eight times, one of which was in an urban district. While the school system was kept under a tight financial restraint by the city, it did receive substantial moral and psychological support from the mayor. He was respected as a friend and maintained high visibility in the local schools.

I had heard that he had a number of relatives working for the school system, including an immediate family member, but I did not appreciate the extent of his network until I inquired. A significant number of teachers were relatives—that is, as we could best determine. The number did not include relatives whose names would be different or who were far enough down the food chain to not be as obvious. Conservatively, we are talking here about forty or more relatives.

It is possible that each one of the relatives was the superior candidate in each of the searches to fill the vacant position, but a reasonable person would certainly not be faulted for questioning such odds. How did it happen that the school system was so generous to members of one family, all of whom were related to a major political player? Is it reasonable to assume that there was some pressure applied, no matter how subtle? Did governing board members ever question this coincidence? Did the superintendents who served over two decades understand what was happening? Were these hirings justified by the fact that the mayor was supportive of the schools, even if not financially generous? If one agrees that this is no mere coincidence, would a log of contacts made to administrators and governing board members outside of the formal guidelines have helped to disclose such practices? In my experience, without the superintendent serving as guardian of the recruiting process, the system will undoubtedly fail.

Chapter 4 reinforces an important recruiting principle: the superintendent is the primary advocate for developing and maintaining integrity in the recruiting process.

4

ADVOCATE FOR EXCELLENCE

OPERATIONAL RESPONSIBILITY

The size of a school district determines who has the operational responsibility for the recruiting program. The larger the district, the more complex the program. The number of personnel in an urban district's human relations department dwarfs that of the entire teaching and administrative staff of a small rural district.

The number of applications received in a large city district in a single year is greater than the number submitted to a suburban district for several years. Hundreds of teachers and administrators are employed in a large district, as compared to a handful in rural areas and a dozen or more in suburban areas. It is obvious that the structure of a human relations department varies greatly as one moves from a large urban district to a typical suburban district to a rural district. The geographic size of a district also influences how recruiting is carried out. In some districts, the superintendent can easily visit all schools in an hour or two, while in other districts, such as those in Alaska, one may need an aircraft to visit schools.

Because of these variables, this chapter does not attempt to describe the organizational structure of an effective human relations department.

The variables are infinite, and no two districts, even those of similar size and demographics, will operate in the same manner. Therefore, this chapter addresses the philosophy of recruiting and not the organizational structure of the recruiting department.

THE ADVOCATE FOR EXCELLENCE

In previous chapters, I emphasized that the superintendent is singularly responsible for the functioning of the recruiting program, regardless of district demographics. The larger the district, the more distant she or he is from the operational aspect; the smaller the district, the closer the superintendent is to the action. In fact, no activity is so vital in terms of effecting positive change in a district as that of attracting outstanding teachers and administrators. The leader of every district must be the primary advocate for excellence in hiring, regardless of size, ethnic or racial makeup, political structure, denominational factors, or financial resources. Organizationally, and depending on size, superintendents may delegate the function to one or more administrators, but their responsibility can never be delegated. The *Titanic* hit an iceberg while the captain was asleep!

What is the basis for establishing excellence in recruiting? What is the basis on which new hires should be judged? What form do assessments take? What makes for excellence in teaching? What does one look for in administrators? None of these questions can be answered unless the superintendent articulates the mission for the recruiting process. The essential question is, What are the philosophical underpinnings for recruitment?

During my thirty-five years of recruiting, I operated with a single philosophical underpinning: every person hired had to possess the skills to raise the average ability of the staff in the specific area in which the new hire was employed. A newly hired teacher of high school English, for example, must be better educated and more qualified than the average member of the English department. That is the minimum to expect. To expect other than that results in a decrease in the average competence level of English department members. As simple a concept as this may be, it is rarely utilized as the basis for hiring. Irrespective of the amount of paperwork generated or the number of interviews held, most new employees are evaluated on a two-point scale: they are either qualified or not qualified! The unfortunate consequences of this attitude is that a new hire who is judged as "qualified" may still be less talented than the average teacher in the English department. If so, the leader has begun the process of undermining, rather than underpinning, the district! A superintendent committed to excellence in hiring understands perfectly well that the English teacher should not only be better than the average teacher in the department but should clearly demonstrate the promise to be the most outstanding of them all.

When recruiting efforts fail to yield a good crop of candidates, many superintendents fall back on excuses such as "There is the shortage in the marketplace" or "I have a salary schedule that is not competitive." Both expressions fail to address the underlying causes for being unable to recruit top-notch employees. In chapter 1, the case was made that the superintendent must be an advocate for improvements in negotiating contracts with teachers and administrators, the results of which make it possible for a superintendent to recruit effectively.

It is relatively easy to qualify for certification as a teacher, administrator, or superintendent. It amounts to little more than acquiring course credits. Moreover, the acquisition of graduate credits is as easy as applying for a driver's license! Unfortunately, of those who receive certification, only a small fraction become outstanding teachers or educational administrators. As mentioned in the introduction, graduate courses in education have served to make our profession the butt of professional jokes. Other professionals, for the most part, do not hold educators in high esteem. State bureaucracies have misled the public into thinking that certification denotes qualification! I have interviewed hundreds of candidates who have the required certification but who lack the ability to teach or lead.

A gifted leader views recruiting as a multidimensional effort that begins with negotiated contracts and a strong commitment from a governing board. What a district saves on salaries, it spends many times over in trying to improve the performance of those who do not have the talent to improve! One of the reasons this multidimensional effort has not caught on in most districts is due to the short tenure of superintendents (often political causalities) who rarely remain in a district long enough to make a difference.

A school district that hires poorly should not place the blame on the human relations department or personnel. The road to improvement in the quality of staff is the mission of the superintendent. When a recruiting system fails, the responsibility for such failure rests with the superintendent, not with human relations personnel. The old school of administration preached the principle that the supervisor, in this case the superintendent, was always responsible for whatever failings occurred in every department in a district. The new school, most often referred to as site-based management, has provided superintendents with an excuse to point fingers at other administrators when things go awry. Holding impromptu trials is a common pastime of marginally competent superintendents.

CONFLICTING INTERESTS

If establishing an effective recruiting program is so vital to the success of a school system, why it is that school leaders tend to focus their interests elsewhere? One can paint the walls, move the filing cabinets, change the drapes in the office, place diplomas on the wall, publish extensively, give inspiring speeches, consult to other districts, transfer personnel, take on adjunct professor roles, sit on committees, and be president of the Rotary; but all of these activities are wastes of time and human resources when a system fails to improve the lives of students. Most of these activities contribute nothing to the mission of the schools, which is to guarantee that all children learn. Short-timers and inward-looking leaders engage in meaningless "reform." As a breed, most superintendents envision themselves as experts in many arenas, yet many are stumped as to how to improve teaching and enhance learning. Most fail to confront state legislatures or commissioners of education except through innocuous professional organizations. Superintendent heroes are in short supply.

We have superintendents who, instead of addressing the No Child Left Behind mission, have chosen to admit defeat and turn down federal money as a way to avoid suffering penalties when they fail to meet the standards. Admitting defeat should not be one of the strategies superintendents employ. One cannot help but wonder what these men and women use as criteria to hire teachers and administrators!

Successful superintendents, those serious about improvement, understand that it is the new hires who most profoundly influence the teaching and learning environment over the long haul. Identifying them and hiring them is a noble cause. Implementing an effective recruiting system requires a leader who offers a long-range vision rather than one who seeks short-term publicity.

Once in place, the recruiting system must guard against bias and prejudice, the topic of chapter 5.

5

SO WHAT IF I'M ITALIAN
AND CATHOLIC?

THE HUMBLING IMPACT OF BIAS AND PREJUDICE

It is impossible for the average educator to experience the humbling impact that racial, religious, and ethnic prejudice have in the workplace. As a white superintendent, I never feel the humiliation often heaped on minority candidates when they are rejected based on color. Most superintendents never personally experience ethnic or religious prejudice. Yet it exists, and superintendents and those they appoint to operate a recruiting program need to be sensitive to the often subtle and occasionally not-so-subtle activities and comments that result in the creation of an uneven playing field for some candidates. Once again, the superintendent is responsible.

The closest I came to experiencing how it feels to be denied equal access to a job opportunity is through the events of the following two anecdotes. While I am not a minority by race or color, in both experiences I was the minority in terms of ethnicity and religion. I share the anecdotes in the hope that no other person applying for a teaching or an administrative position will have similar experiences. Bias and prejudice in hiring are not only shameful acts but criminal ones.

I precede the following two anecdotes with the definitions of *bias* and *prejudice*. *Bias* is a "highly personal and unreasoned distortion of judgment," and *prejudice* is an "adverse opinion or leaning without just grounds or before sufficient knowledge." Both anecdotes drive home the ugly message that prejudice and bias are always at play and that men and women in leadership roles must fight for fair play in recruiting at every opportunity. It is a battle they must wage each day. If leaders do not rise to the occasion, then who will?

ANECDOTE NUMBER I

I had been appointed to an administrative position in a small seacoast community. The demographics were such that most of the wealthy landowners, shipbuilders, marina owners, entrepreneurs, and the moneyed and famous families who resided in the community sent their children to private schools after the fifth or eighth grade. The students who remained were, for the most part, from families who were employed in the shipyards, marinas, and small businesses in town, or they were children of those who commuted to Boston for work. Most were from blue-collar or middle-class families. The schools were average. My training with outstanding mentors made this a perfect assignment, or so I thought. The superintendent who hired me was highly regarded, and that proved to be a blessing.

There were very few Italians living in the community, and I was the first Roman Catholic (and the first Italian) to be appointed to an administrative position. At the outset, I was not aware of this distinction, nor would I have refused the position if I had known. During the transition to the new position, I spent several half days in the community. On one of those days, I went for a walk through the town center and stopped into a small shop that sold candy, newspapers, and greeting cards. It was located on Main Street in the midst of several other small shops. It could be described as quaint. The owner was a woman who had lived in town her entire life. Shortly after I entered to make a purchase, she said she recognized me by my picture that had recently been published by the local weekly. There were a few minutes of informal chitchat when, unexpectedly, she inquired as to my nationality! As offensive as the question was, I mistakenly decided not to do battle on my first visit downtown. In retrospect, I made a poor decision in responding. I can only blame it on inexperience and being caught off guard. I never, in a thousand years, would have expected the question.

I replied that I was Italian on both my mother's side and my father's side. She stunned me with her response: "Thank God you're not Greek!" It was obvious that if I told her I was Greek, she would have retorted with "Thank God you're not Italian" or whatever other ethnic group came into mind. Clearly, she wanted no "ethnic types" in "her" community and left little doubt about it. She wanted to be in charge of the drawbridge and decide was who qualified to cross the moat. She was the standard bearer. What she expressed with her comment was an "adverse opinion or leaning without just grounds or before sufficient knowledge."

Thankfully, she did not represent community sentiments. Among the sad aspects of this exchange was the fact that literally around the corner from her business was a highly successful Greek restaurant that had been in the community for many years. (The food at the restaurant, by the way, was authentic, inexpensive, and spectacular).

ANECDOTE NUMBER 2

I applied for a position in a small, wealthy, exclusive New Hampshire community for an entry-level administrative position. What I did not know at the time was that a social and professional friend of mine had also applied for the same position. My friend is Scottish, English, and Protestant. As noted earlier, I am Italian and Catholic. He was afforded an interview and was ultimately appointed to the position. The district never acknowledged my application, nor did it inform me that another person had been hired. When my friend told me of his good fortune, I related to him my experience in having applied and my not having heard from the district at either the beginning or end of the process. I paraphrase his reply: "Do you really think that this essentially English, Protestant community would appoint a Catholic, let alone an Italian?"

I was naïve enough in the youth of my career to believe that a community would be open to the best-qualified candidate. While every candidate wants to believe he or she is the better candidate, my professional record was clearly superior in this case, but I was never provided even the opportunity to present it to the school committee. It adopted "an adverse opinion or leaning without just grounds or before sufficient knowledge."

These two very painful encounters have remained with me through all the years of my public school experience and during my decade of consulting. Today, I realize that bias and prejudice are all too alive and well. Perhaps they are more subtle today, but they are nonetheless destructive. In both small and big ways, and every day and everywhere, unfair practices take place. If bias and prejudice are not at play, then it is patronage and favoritism. No matter, it all washes out dirty.

One way to ensure that interviewers can handle issues of bias and prejudice is by proper training, the contents of chapter 6.

6

KNOWING THE QUESTIONS

If your district wants to be competitive in hiring outstanding educators, your interviewers need to know what to ask, when to ask it, how to ask it, and to whom to ask it! A failure to be thorough in questioning is an invitation for serious trouble to pay you a visit.

Before interviewers are in a position to "ask" anything, they need to be trained. Interviewing candidates effectively is a skill that few administrators, teachers, or community representatives possess. As a superintendent for twenty-five years and a consultant for more than twelve, I have witnessed hundreds of interviews conducted by both school personnel and laypeople. Many of those interviews failed to raise questions that would have gathered valuable information or that would have provided an accurate insight into the personality or teaching/leadership style of the candidates.

Most interviewers are inept at interviewing because they come to the process without any specialized training. Most superintendents operate on the assumption that once an educator is certified as an administrator or teacher, he or she is automatically qualified to be an interviewer. The assumption extends to those who lead parent groups. My experience tells me otherwise. The fact is that the hiring agent needs to take as much time selecting interviewers as in selecting candidates! Employees should not be allowed anywhere near a candidate for the purpose of interviewing without their having previously engaged in professional training.

TRAINING OF INTERVIEWERS

Before my work as an educator, I worked in military intelligence and served with a counterintelligence unit of the army. I underwent several months of training before being assigned overseas as a military investigator. While on assignment, I received intensive on-the-job training from outstanding, experienced, proficient field agents. I was awestruck by the level of competency of these men, some of whom regularly penetrated the iron curtain to collect valuable information.

Although the physical aspect of the training was demanding, the most challenging part of the training was the interviewing aspect. Failure to master this skill was the primary reason candidates washed out of the program. When I think back on the training, I recall the stress all of us endured as the moment arrived when we had to conduct final interviews and interrogations before an audience of experienced military agents who had worked in the field and who would decide which of the candidates would continue in the program. It is important to note that not all of those in training would be assigned to undercover roles in foreign countries, which is the assignment that most agents desired. Many of those in training would ultimately be assigned to routine investigative assignments in the United States, where most of their time would be spent conducting routine background checks on individuals applying for government employment or their references. Many of the subjects being interviewed were already in the employ of the government, and background checks were being conducted to determine if they were eligible for a higher or different security clearance. Yet the military deemed this routine investigative work to be sufficiently important to warrant extensive training for its agents. Why then, when we are employing teachers and administrators who shape the lives of our children, do we provide literally no training for the interviewers responsible for selecting candidates? What little we do offer in the way of training to educators who are engaged in interviewing is very different from the emphasis and importance that the military places on quality training.

UNSKILLED INTERVIEWERS

From experience, the military recognized that whatever time marginally competent investigators spend interviewing friendly personnel or interrogating hostile individuals was of little value if the agent or agents were unskilled. Unskilled investigators usually acquired useless information or became party to disinformation or misinformation. This is the reason the military washes out a large number of its candidates for military intelligence assignments. But education never washes out any of its interviewers! Alternatively, if the interviewers are highly skilled, they are able to collect valuable information, both with and without the awareness of those being interviewed. Unskilled and unqualified interviewers working for a public school district collect useless information, act on that information, and succeed in placing incompetent teachers and administrators in classrooms and boardrooms.

DAMAGE CONTROL

I am unable to recall any formal training I received in education that has remained with me for so many years and that was so valuable in my roles as building principal and central office administrator than that of interviewing candidates. As a superintendent, I worked with literally hundreds of talented educators in joint efforts to build a highly respected school system. They were selected after undergoing extensive interviews and background checks. As a consultant whose career success was directly related to the quality of candidates I presented to a governing board, I could not have survived without excellent interviewing skills.

In *Job Hunting in Education*, there are many references to the need for hiring agents to be well trained in the recruiting process, for to do otherwise is a disservice to candidates. The present book points the finger at the hiring agent, the most important of whom is the superintendent, as the one person who can make or break a school system. Until and unless those who interview are properly trained, then it is fair to assume that those who are employed by those not trained in the selection process are poor choices.

Where does a governing board come into play? The answer is quite simple. A governing board must demand the highest possible standards for interviewers; otherwise, the money for salaries is wasted on marginally competent employees or average employees who have little chance of improving and who are unable to meet the highest standard of performance. Public schools expend far too much time attempting to improve the performance of marginal employees when the time would have better spent training those who do the hiring. Is it any wonder that the public balks at annual incremental pay for less-than-outstanding teachers and administrators? Why is anyone surprised when school budgets are defeated?

WHAT MAKES FOR SUCCESSFUL TRAINING

What was it that the military did so successfully? First, it screened candidates entering its program and established the highest expectations for those accepted into the program. Once in, candidates were able to succeed because of the professional development provided to them. I came close to washing out due to poor writing skills. I attribute that to incompetent high school teachers who ignored kids from ethnic neighborhoods whose foreign language–speaking immigrant parents were not able to assist them. Those days are different from the situation today, wherein non-English-speaking students are provided with significant federal-mandated assistance. The struggle of today's non-English-speaking students pales next to what immigrants faced in the late nineteenth and early twentieth centuries.

My struggle with English continued into college, and it abated only when a college professor provided me with some tutoring. Once accepted into the military intelligence program, I was provided one-on-one writing assistance as part of my training. Both experiences prove the point that training is critical to successful performance. In my case, the training was essential in the area of writing. For other candidates in the military program, assistance was needed in the interviewing process.

USE OF PROFESSIONAL TRAINERS

As soon as superiors were convinced that the candidates could handle the academics, the military initiated interview training. It is from my experience that today's superintendents can learn a lesson about training interviewers. This section addresses only the interviewing aspect of the training. There is absolutely no justification to use interrogation techniques during the recruiting process. Most of the interviewees (those being interviewed) the military employed were professional actors and actresses who were skilled in working with agents in training. Experienced agents also acted out some of the roles of interviewees. The agents in training played the roles of the interviewers, and initially, they were no match for the professionally trained interviewees. The uneducated were being challenged by the educated.

The actors, actresses, and military agents assumed many roles and exploited the weaknesses of the interviewers. They toyed with the agents in training. It was like a cat-and-mouse game. They would be evasive. They could be noncommittal. They could be deceptive, or they could be open. They could be resistant or cooperative. The fact is that they worked an interviewer to see how responsive he or she was to the subtleties of words and experience. Their goal was to make the interviewers work for every scrap of information. They had no compunction about lying, deceiving, confusing, or frustrating interviewers. The role of the interviewee in a training session is to make the inexperienced interviewer work at fact-finding. The goal is to develop outstanding interviewers.

WHO RECEIVED THE ALLOTTED INTERVIEW TIME?

One of the guiding rules of interviewing is for the interviewer to provide the interviewees with 90 percent of the talking time and leave 10 percent to himself or herself. It is in the talking by the interviewees that something of value is discovered about their style, personality, ethics, and qualifications. In a training session, the interviewee attempts to turn the tables by having the interviewer do most of the talking, thus providing little time for the interviewer to learn much about the interviewee! Once again, experience tells me that interviewers love to talk.

My experience with talking time is based on thirty-five years of working with administrators and teachers and with private clients. Most interviewers love to talk about themselves during an interview. Take, for example, a situation where a superintendent is interviewing a candidate for an administrative position. The candidate is asked, "What is the toughest issue you were confronted with this year?" The answer: "It was in dealing with a board member who in a roundabout manner suggested that I should get his child into the National Honor Society." Rather than follow up on the answer to acquire more detail, the superintendent responds with, "As a principal I can remember a similar situation when the mayor. . . ." Following the lead of the superintendent, the candidate appropriately shuts down to avoid offending the superintendent and becomes the listener rather than the talker. There are two consequences to this action. First, the candidate loses valuable interviewing time to sell himself or herself; second, the superintendent loses valuable time to learn more about the candidate. In the training of interviewers, one of the guiding principles is that interviewers must learn to be active listeners, which is a polite way of saying that they should learn to be quiet.

This chapter makes the case for the training of interviewers. When incompetents are employed as teachers and administrators because of failures in the recruiting process, the district is always in a damage-control mode. Before your interviewers are qualified to know what to ask, when to ask it, how to ask it, and to whom to ask it, they need to have appropriate training. Chapter 15 provides specific suggestions for an effective interview.

In the chapter that follows, you play sleuth as you hit the paper trail.

7

THE PAPER TRAIL AND
QUALITY OF SERVICE

PAPER TRAIL OF INEXPERIENCED CANDIDATES

One of the lessons learned in military intelligence was the importance of following the paper trail of candidates. When a candidate commits a story to paper, it is fair to assume it is accurate. In many cases it will not be.

In the case of new teachers fresh out of college, the trail is relatively easy to follow. Only four or five years out of high school, they will have had few assignments or professional experiences. Transcripts are recent as are student teaching experiences. References are current and generally include those of university advisors and supervising teachers and administrators. What questions that do arise about their professional lives are easily answered. Questions not so easily answered are those of a personal nature that could influence your hiring decision. For example, you need to determine from the paperwork if a candidate has taken longer than four or five years to complete the undergraduate degree, and if so, why? Are there breaks in employment? As noted elsewhere in this guide, it is vital that the application and resume account for every month of every year beginning with the date the student graduated from high school. If candidates list only years of employment or education, you need to require them to revise their applications to account for every month of every year. Why is this so important? For one thing, you want to determine if candidates may have encountered some difficulty with the law. You also want to know if they were temporarily employed during the missing period and what is it they were employed doing. You do not want to be the last person to learn that a candidate was employed as a topless dancer, part-time or not! While that would not disqualify a candidate from employment, the employer needs to know what may be in store for the school system if the media discover this fact. The lesson learned is that failure to complete a thorough historical check of a candidate's past could lead to hiring someone who has something in his or her background that could embarrass the district.

PAPER TRAIL OF EXPERIENCED CANDIDATES

When dealing with the paper trail of experienced teachers and administrators, there is significantly more risk in ignoring it. As is the case with an inexperienced candidate, there is an imperative to fill in all gaps in a candidate's history by making him or her account for every month since leaving high school. To some this may appear to be overkill, but to an experienced consultant, it is baseline information. The following information is an extract from a section from my first book, *Job Hunting in Education: An Insider's Guide to Success*. It illustrates the necessity of questioning any time gaps in a candidate's history.

Examples of Incomplete Records

As a candidate, you must be particularly careful about how you record dates of employment. If you use only full years, without months, you have the opportunity to literally hide an entire year or more. For example, consider the following employment dates for this candidate:

1991–1992	Worked in District A
1992–1995	Worked in District B
1995–2002	Worked in District C

At first glance, it appears that the candidate had been employed continuously from 1991 through 1992 in District A. However, he or she could have worked from December 1991 to January 1992, a period of only two months!

Similarly, he or she could have worked from December 1992 to January 1995 in District B, a total of twenty-six months instead of the forty-eight months that is implied in using the dates 1992–1995.

While on a consulting assignment wherein I was hiring several administrators for the same district, I came across an application submitted for an assistant superintendent position. The application caught my attention because of the manner in which the applicant recorded his experiences. It was similar to the format just illustrated. He recorded the years and not the months. I remembered him as having had a very short career as a superintendent in another state. While I did not know him personally, I knew the name and the circumstances of his employment and subsequent unemployment. He had been released from his contract before the end of his first year as superintendent. On his new application he did as just described in an attempt to hide a ten-month assignment that had ended badly. I scheduled an interview with him and asked him if he had ever been employed as a superintendent. He answered no. For all practical purposes, his job search with this district was over.

The extract noted here and that was included in *Job Hunting in Education* was written as a warning to candidates to be careful in recording dates of education and employment. It is also a warning to recruiters to be diligent in accounting for a candidate's entire work history. The extract is included here as a strong reminder to hiring agents to follow the paper trail of both experienced and inexperienced candidates.

After many years of experience, I can attest to the fact that a significant percentage of candidates do not accurately report their histories in terms of the time sequence requested on applications. Many have things to hide that, while not criminal in nature, could be personally and professionally embarrassing to the candidate and the district. A school system has no business intruding into the bedrooms of its candidates, but candidates need to be honest about their past. Integrity is essential in the character of teachers and administrators who work with children. It is for the employer to decide, within the parameters of the law, whether an indiscretion (or worse) would impede a candidate's work in the district.

However, if as the employing agent you do not engage in due diligence, then you deserve what you get. The previous chapter emphasizes the necessity to utilize skilled interviewers, those capable of addressing matters such as this. If you do not ask, you will not learn. As the person conducting this phase of a background check, you cannot be reluctant to ask tough questions. You either embarrass yourself now or compromise yourself later. You cannot have it both ways!

Incomplete Applications

In many cases candidates are simply negligent in completing applications. This omission may tell you something about a candidate. When the employing agent designs an application form, it is with the expectation that a candidate will complete it accurately and in its entirety; otherwise, why have an application? The following are examples of how six semifinalists for a superintendent position handled their applications. These could just as well be applications for teaching and principal positions.

Four were superintendents and two were assistant superintendents. I want to note that a cover letter, in my opinion, is an essential part of an application and can do much to assist a candidate in moving forward in the process.

All were required to submit the following:

Cover letter
A single-sheet, two-sided application
A current resume
Three current letters of recommendation from those who could speak to the professional work of the candidate
The names, addresses, and phone numbers of three additional references
Transcripts for all academic work beyond high school
Copy of superintendent certification for the state of application
Fifteen copies of a two- or three-page document created in the course of their work as an example of writing ability

The following is the record of how the six candidates responded.

Candidate Number 1
Submitted ten letters of reference rather than three.
A writing sample was submitted that was assessed as damaging to the candidate.
All dates were by year and not by months.

Candidate Number 2
Initially, no resume submitted.
Resume, when finally received, was in a format that could not be copied.
Seven letters of reference; one was fourteen years old, another ten years old.

Candidate Number 3
Unimpressive and poorly written cover letter.
No letter of reference from the immediate supervisor.
Inappropriate letters of reference.
Did not provide names and phone numbers of three additional references.

Candidate Number 4
Poorly written cover letter that distracted from candidacy.
Several key sections of application were left blank and stated, "See attachment."
Writing sample was in the form of several major promotional booklets.

Candidate Number 5
All teaching and administrative experience listed only by years.
Listed several pages of outside affiliations without any dates.

Candidate Number 6
Several key sections of application stated, "See attachment."
All dates were by years and not months.

While on the surface, these omissions may not appear to be important defects, yet they place the responsibility on the recruiter to unearth data that should have been provided by candidates. In other words, the recruiter ends up doing the work of the candidate! These omissions by the candidates cause the process to bog down as the district waits for relevant documents to be submitted or applications to be edited by the candidates. More important, these applications were submitted by so-called leaders of a district, who are expected to set high standards. They failed to meet entry-level standards for a job application. Experience has proven that most efforts to address these concerns with candidates are not welcomed.

QUALITY OF SERVICE

Once your examination of the paper trail has been completed and you are satisfied that the candidate has accurately represented himself or herself and that all doubts have been eliminated, it is time to assess the quality of the service listed on the application and recorded on transcripts. This is one of the two most sensitive aspects of the recruiting process. The second important aspect is a background check to determine if the candidate has a hidden past or a professional or personal experience that can bring discredit to the candidate and the district if the past were to become known publicly. Those who conduct either of the background checks, one to determine quality of service and the other to check on a hidden past, must have finely honed investigative skills.

In determining quality of service, the hiring agent needs to recognize other aspects of a person's career in addition to his or her primary teaching or administrative service. These other areas include:

Professional affiliations
Selected accomplishments
Professional contributions and writings
Awards received
Civic contributions
Other interests
Seeking top performers

While none of the above substitute for outstanding teaching or administrative experience, they serve as a way for the hiring agent to make distinctions among several outstanding candidates. Candidates who engage in activities beyond their normal school assignment are demonstrating personal and professional initiative, a desired characteristic for those in public education.

One of the essential questions to be raised of every candidate is, What have you done this week in your present assignment that distinguishes you from all of the other candidates for this position? In other words, how do you as a recruiter separate this candidate from the pack? Unless a candidate has been willing to step up and volunteer for assignments in his or her current position that others forgo, it is most likely he or she will not step up after being hired. One of the lessons that inexperienced superintendents and consultants learn, occasionally the hard way, is that the majority of us do not change our attitudes as a result of changing jobs. We are who we are, and unless we are placed under duress or threatened with job loss, we will continue to perform in the same manner. Even then, the minute supervisory pressure is removed from a nonperformer, he or she will revert to old habits. It is for this reason that background checks are so vital. Just as SATs are one effective predictor of success in college, along with class rank, grade point average, and recommendations, so it is that "what a person has been in the past" is a fairly accurate predictor of what he or she will be in the future. There are, of course, exceptions, but they are just that, exceptions! Hiring agents must not rely on long odds or luck in the recruiting process. They need to have solid assurance that they are employing top performers. How do they know that?

Everyone Has a History

Regardless of what position in education a candidate applies for, he or she has a professional history. Even a graduate student, applying for a first-time position, has a history of performance in high school, undergraduate school, part-time employment, and as a student teacher or teacher aide. At the other end of the experience spectrum, a very experienced superintendent has a long history of experiences. In either case, a background check to determine quality of performance is equally important. How does one go about assessing quality of performance?

Assessing Quality of Service

Having worked with many administrators who participated in the interviewing and background checks aspects of recruiting, I can state with certainly that there was a significant difference in their abilities. There were administrators in whom I had the highest level of confidence in terms of their ability to check out a candidate's background. They did this by contacting appropriate persons qualified to speak to a candidate's ability. They knew the questions to ask, when to follow up, when to be skeptical, and when to start anew. If any doubt existed, they knew how to rework the conversation to delve more deeply into a candidate's background. They were not diverted from the task by a candidate's appearance or personality. When these administrators turned in their assessments, I had confidence that I could move forward with my final interviews and ultimately extend a contract of employment to one of the finalists without concern.

Five Hurdles to Success   Other administrators, outstanding at their primary job, did not possess the skills needed to interview effectively or conduct background checks. I did not select them to make decisions unilaterally; rather, they were assigned to group interviews, where their opinions were factored into a group decision and where they could witness effective interviewing techniques. To allow them to be the primary interviewer or to be in charge of background checks would be a disservice to the district and to the candidates.

If we assume that a candidate has an excellent teaching or administrative record, what other factors go into making a final decision to hire him or her? For twenty-five years, I used the same rating scale to judge the "other" factors that were important to my district and me. I believe they are still relevant to all districts today and are as appropriate for the beginning teacher as they are for the experienced administrator. The following section is taken from a chapter written for beginning teachers in *Job Hunting in Education*. However, during my career, I employed the identical scale to judge candidates applying for any professional position.

First, I assess the degree to which I believe a candidate is able to handle crisis immediately. Education is a profession in which crisis lurks around each corner. Whether it is an accident on the playground, a life-threatening food-allergy emergency, a young child missing from school, students harassing one another, or an abusive student, a teacher needs the skills to respond appropriately and effectively.

Second, I need evidence of a candidate's ability to manage. While we accept as a matter of fact that administrators need to possess outstanding management skills, we often fail to recognize that the modern teacher assignment is filled with management demands. Good management skills are required when handling test score data, student assignments, attendance records, and general classroom activities. The paper burden on teachers has grown each year.

Third, I want evidence of a candidate's high level of effective interpersonal skills. Education is a people business, and a teacher needs to possess the ability to interact effectively and responsibly with students, parents, staff, and administration. Many teachers with outstanding academic records and classroom successes have failed because of an inability to interact with other adults.

Fourth, I am interested in a candidate's poise and carriage and the messages they send. Nonverbal messages are as powerful as spoken and written ones. The way one carries oneself projects to others whether one is a teacher of confidence or one who is insecure. Before you even utter your first word when meeting parents, they will quickly, for better or worse, make a judgment about you based on your body language.

Fifth, I look for a candidate who has potential for growth. No school system is ever satisfied with what a new teacher learned during the undergraduate or student teacher experiences. Those alone are not adequate for the long-term classroom demands. Therefore, the candidate must possess the will and ability to continue with formal education and be an active participant in local professional development activities. Every new teacher should have the potential to become a mentor to others.

The five standards listed here should be important to all hiring agents. The standards help employers distinguish among the candidates in making final judgments.

Evidence of Quality

Assessing a candidate's prior and current quality of service is the most essential part of the paper trail investigation. Every district views quality according to its own standard. There are, however, at least three areas I always investigated. If satisfied with what I learned, it was a rare case wherein the candidate was not successful once employed in my district.

Area Number 1   A recruiter must have evidence that a candidate was successful at every position held no matter how small or insignificant the position. It is the history of success that is vital, not the title of the position held. What a candidate will accomplish professionally in the future will reflect where she or he has been professionally. If there are one or two occasions in an otherwise successful career where success seemed to have eluded the candidate, you need to have a full understanding of why this occurred and learn why it was out of character. It is not unusual to find a negative situation that was beyond the control of a candidate. On balance, however, you seek a candidate whose career comprises successful assignments. The recruiting motto must be "Nothing succeeds like success."

Area Number 2   A recruiter must have evidence that a candidate has worked successfully with other professionals at every level of an organization. This includes staff in support positions, such as custodians, secretaries, clerks, paraprofessionals, and others in the organization usually referred to as noncertified to distinguish them from those who possess teacher and administrator certifications. I know of a school system where the superintendent decided to make a site visit to the district where a candidate he was interested in for a vice principal position in his district was employed as a teacher. The superintendent arrived, and other than having a few words with the candidate's principal, he spent the entire morning talking with students, secretaries, custodians, clerks, and other support staff to gather important information about the candidate. Why did the superintendent spend so much time conversing with support staff? Clearly, he placed great value on a candidate's interpersonal relations with staff members at all levels of the organization. Highly honed interpersonal skills are an intelligence that recruiters should seek in all candidates.

Area Number 3   Finally, a recruiter needs to gather evidence that a candidate was among the first, if not the first, to volunteer to take on extra tasks in his or her school district. It is an important way for a candidate to stand out from the crowd. Most educators do what they have to do; few do more than is expected. It is the latter that a recruiter seeks to employ. If someone has not distinguished himself or herself in the current position, why would a recruiter expect other than that after the person is hired?

Pursuing the paper trail for inconsistencies and investigating a candidate's quality of service are important aspects of the hiring process. It is a dull task and hard work. It does not differ much from the work of a private detective who spends a good deal of investigative time with mundane details. It is from the many details that a story is written. Without a complete story, recruiters are at a serious disadvantage when judging candidates.

Now on to chapter 8, "Your Haunting Past," where we explore the potentially dark side of a candidate. Without wanting to do so, you may be entering murky waters!

8

YOUR HAUNTING PAST

Chapter 7 provides information on what to look for when conducting a background check into a candidate's past. It also provides advice on how to determine a candidate's quality of service. Background checking is a relatively easy task if it is assigned to administrators who are skilled at the process. It is also a very important task since without a guarantee that a candidate's service has been outstanding, a district runs the risk of diminishing the average quality of its staff. There are always a sufficient number of marginal candidates available in the marketplace; therefore, it is easy enough for a district to fill all of its vacancies. Many districts are satisfied just to claim a body to put into a classroom. These are generic-brand districts with average or below-average expectations for both staff and students. A district may easily join this group by simply failing to install a quality, aggressive, professional recruiting system. One certain way to do this is to fail to conduct a complete and comprehensive background check. For example, when searching for principals, a recruiter needs to understand that principals constitute a universe of their own, and any one administrator falls somewhere on a bell curve when it comes to positive or negative human behavior. They are no different from any other group of professionals. They can be as unethical and immoral as any other category of educators. They are just as susceptible to alcohol and drug abuse as others are. They have been known to embezzle funds or engage in extramarital affairs. In short, they are human and subject to human frailties. The job of the recruiter is to conduct a background check that provides answers that justify your giving clearance to a candidate much as the government does in granting security clearances to its employees.

What are the areas of concern that should be the focus of a routine investigation into a person's background? What approach should a recruiter take? What should the candidate expect?

As a private search consultant, I represent a school district in any given search; consequently, I use extreme caution in checking out the backgrounds of candidates. I am particularly sensitive since I have been burned twice and singed several times because of vital information that candidates withheld. In two cases, the issue centered on an extramarital affair that the superintendent had with a member of his own governing board. Affairs of this nature are explosive when revealed. During the period when this manuscript was being prepared, I received an application from a candidate applying for a superintendent position. After conducting a preliminary check, I found that he was driven from his current job because of one such affair.

In an effort to uncover indiscretions early in the process, I conclude my interview with a candidate with one simple but provocative question: "Is there anything in your personal or professional background, which if it were to become known publicly, would bring disgrace to you and embarrassment to me and to the potential employer?" It is a tough question but a fair question as long as you ask it of every candidate, without exception, and regardless whether you know the candidate personally or professionally. As a recruiter, you cannot answer for a candidate, which is what you do by not asking the question; rather, you need to hear her or him provide an answer to the question. Each has a slightly different view of what constitutes "disgrace" and "embarrassment," but all are intelligent enough to know that certain activities in one's past may come back to haunt a person if made known publicly.

Some candidates share experiences they believe to be a problem, but to the interviewer they may not be perceived as an issue. Others explain a situation that they believe is not an issue but to the interviewer is considered an obstacle that cannot be overcome. In both cases, the recruiter makes a judgment call. Depending on what decision is made, the candidate may be dropped from consideration or may be moved ahead pending a more thorough background check.

The problem arises when a candidate, in response to the essential question, answers untruthfully or uses words to misinform the interviewer. It is at this point that a skilled interviewer needs to be a careful listener, being tuned to inconsistencies and sensitive to lapses in time or places. On many occasions, I have initially ignored questionable or inconsistent responses only to return to them at a different point in the interview. By doing so, I have caught candidates off guard, sometimes with it showing in their obvious embarrassment or in their losing traction in the interview.

Digging deep into a candidate's background is difficult work. Often, when you have what appears to be an outstanding candidate, there is a tendency to ease off on checks. This is a poor policy. If nothing else, the checks are comforting to the employer about to extend a contract. I offer my most recent case as an example. Again, during the period this manuscript was being prepared, I was involved in a superintendent search, the same as mentioned earlier in which a candidate was involved in an extramarital affair. I quickly eliminated him from the process. However, the finalist for the position had passed all three of the interviews with flying colors and was the candidate of choice pending the completion of a site visit and background check, the latter being left for me to conduct. One or two phone calls would have been sufficient given other information we possessed about this candidate. Nevertheless, I contacted five professionals, all of whom possessed detailed knowledge of his work and successes. All validated what we already knew. It took the equivalent of four hours to complete and record those five conversations and an additional hour to prepare a report for my client. Some recruiters would consider the time I spent on the comprehensive background check an unnecessary expenditure of time and money. I considered it an investment to secure a human asset of considerable value. I still insisted that the client make a site visit to the candidate's home community to further validate my findings. The lesson for recruiters is that you can never be too careful. Every time you are about to offer a contract of employment, you must remind yourself that you are doing so on behalf of children who are staking their lives on the quality of your work!

This chapter identifies the several areas that can cause upheaval in the recruiting process. From experience, I have encountered all of them. Each carries its own virus that can weaken both a candidate and a school district. Candidates want jobs, and some will act unethically and deceitfully to gain employment. Recruiters need candidates, but they must also be unrelenting in pursuing the truth about a candidate regardless of where it leads. In another life, you can be counselor and therapist, but as the recruiter responsible for the education of children, you are now an investigator and assessor of talent. Nothing must interfere with your mission. So often, those in support positions, such as human relations personnel, do not appreciate the degree to which they are responsible for the actions of teachers and administrators who are unsuccessful and subsequently fail children. It may be a long distance, physically, emotionally, and psychologically, from the central office interviewing room to the classroom, but it is only a stone's throw to potential disaster!

A word about the media is worthwhile at this point. There are few individuals as adept at background checking as investigative reporters. While there have always been reporters who loved to be investigators, Watergate became the watershed for in-depth investigation of public figures. Woodward and Bernstein set the pace for every reporter seeking a Pulitzer Prize. After Watergate, newspapers in particular became much more aggressive in pursuing public sector wrongdoing. Earlier, I mentioned that the media would love to discover a high-ranking public sector administrator who is engaged in some wrongdoing, such as using patronage as a way to outflank the formal recruiting process. It is no wonder that they have an interest in who works in or who leads our public schools. A district plays with fire if it brings forth a candidate without having conducted due diligence into her or his background. If there is anything in a candidate's background that is damaging, the chances are that the major newspaper covering your district will know of it before you do. To avoid this situation, you need to be aggressive in conducting your background checks. It is one reason why we do not reveal the names of finalists until we have fulfilled our due diligence requirement. There are ample horror stories about districts that have failed to do so. You must not be one of them.

The following section formed the basis for chapter 4 in *Job Hunting in Education*. The section was written to alert a candidate to what is examined as a school district conducts checks into his background. The material is now recast from the perspective that the recruiter must use in conducting background checks. Understandably, the more experienced the candidates, the more intensive the background checks. The greater the number of positions they have held, the greater the depth and scope of the background checks. The more controversial a career, the more numerous the individuals contacted for confirmation.

CRIMINAL RECORD

When a candidate applies for a position, you must request the completion of a questionnaire inquiring if he or she has an arrest record, whether he or she was ever convicted of a crime, or if there are criminal proceedings pending against him or her. There should be space for the candidate to provide relevant explanations. The governing board's attorney should approve the questionnaire. The questionnaire must make it clear to the candidate that this procedure is in addition to a formal criminal-record check to be conducted once employed. The wording on the questionnaire must make it clear to the candidate that if he or she lies on the application, the district has the legal right to dismiss him or her out of hand.

I strongly suggest that the recruiter employ recruiting documents that have undergone legal scrutiny and approval by the school district's attorney. You must avoid having a candidate bring a lawsuit claiming discrimination based on inappropriate questions asked on an employment application.

If the candidate indicates a criminal record, you have a judgment to make. It may require an opinion from your superintendent and from the district's attorney. For example, you will have candidates who may have attended college during the 1960s and 1970s, when drugs were commonly used both on and off campus. Some may have been arrested and convicted for drug use or campus disruptions. It is also not uncommon to have candidates who had been arrested for driving while under the influence of liquor. The latter can be a serious issue depending on how active antidrinking groups are in the region. As a recruiter, you must decide if the public exposure of an arrest and conviction for a driving-while-intoxicated arrest will create a major issue in the district.

I now present anecdotes of two candidates for whom public exposure of past indiscretions stopped one in his tracks and forced the second to reconsider his next professional move.

In the first case, I worked with an outstanding superintendent who was driven from his position because of a drug possession arrest that took place when he was eighteen years old, some twenty years in his past! This caused what appeared to be a brilliant career to be stopped dead in its tracks. He was employed in a large metropolitan district where dirty politics included destroying a reputation if necessary. I had worked with this candidate on a federal grant many years earlier when he was an elementary school principal. I knew the quality service he had provided, and I respected his talents. After the incident forced him out of his position, he applied for a position in a district where the board was conducting its own search and I was hired to conduct background checks on twelve semifinalists. He was one of the twelve. We discussed his drug arrest and how the public disclosure of it had adversely affected his tenure in another district. To paraphrase the question I asked of him: "What will your reaction be if you are hired and the issue of the drug arrest surfaces once again? Given the toll it took on you the first time, will you be able to manage the negative press?" He thought about it for a few days and then made the decision that he could not hold up emotionally if he had to go through a public debate a second time. He decided to withdraw from the competition. I am certain that if I had brought his name to the governing board, it would have rejected my recommendation, fearful of the public's reaction when full disclosure of his arrest was made public. As a recruiter, you need to be certain that a criminal record does not lurk in a candidate's past.

At the other end of the administrative continuum, I worked with a former assistant high school principal who was forced from his position because of a driving-while-intoxicated arrest. He left the state in which he had been arrested and carved out a successful career in education in another state, attaining the position of assistant superintendent in a large suburban district. He wanted to return to New England and applied through me for a superintendent's position in a town that was within twenty miles of the district in which he had been arrested when he was an assistant principal. It was also within the same circulation area of the major metropolitan newspaper that carried the original story. During our interview, he talked freely about the drinking issue in response to the question "Is there anything in your personal or professional background, which if it were to become known publicly, would bring disgrace to you, or embarrassment to me or to the employer?" He went on to share with me that his moving out of state after his arrest was a good decision. He had been a teacher in the general area and still had a support group. They made it possible for him to start over, an opportunity many do not get.

At the time of my interview with him, it was obvious he was professionally qualified for the superintendent position for which he had applied. Nevertheless, the issue of the drinking incident and the arrest remained. My question to him was "If the drunken driving charge of many years ago is made public, can you stand the adverse and controversial publicity that is bound to occur, especially since MADD [Mothers Against Drunk Driving] had been so actively involved?" To paraphrase, his response was "One time is enough." He withdrew. However, he needed someone to pose the question to him and talk about the consequences of the public exposure of the earlier arrest if it became public a second time. Similar to the first case, I am certain that the governing board would have rejected his application knowing that the newspaper would quickly learn of his past arrest.

The lesson in both cases is that as the recruiter, you must unearth issues such as these before the media learn of them. You need time to consider what your next step is in light of what you have learned, and you need to weigh the impact of your decision on the school district you represent. It is too late to ponder alternatives once the media have done your homework!

I am deeply troubled by the fact that a poor decision made in one's past, sometimes a distant past, can continue to hang over a good candidate like a sword suspended by a thread. Yet the reality is that old errors may plague aspiring and experienced candidates forever. It is a fact that a fingerprinted criminal arrest, not to speak of a conviction, will probably remain with a candidate for life.

LAWSUITS

In addition to requesting information as it pertains to a possible criminal record, districts should also inquire if a candidate has been or is currently involved in any lawsuits as either a defendant or plaintiff. Routine matters should not be of concern to you, but lawsuits that involve a legal dispute between a candidate and a former employer need to be examined. Lawsuits concerning any fiduciary wrongdoing while the candidate worked as a school administrator are also of interest. Some districts are concerned about a candidate's credit rating to determine if financial issues will haunt him or her while in a new position.

I once worked with a candidate who was applying for the position of superintendent of schools in another state and was involved in a lawsuit with a former employer. The details are not important for purposes of this section, but the failure of the candidate to be candid is important. The candidate never informed the board or the consultant about the pending court case. It happened that one board member heard a rumor and pursued it in some detail. He then informed the other board members at a meeting at which I was present. It was new information to me!

As it happened, the candidate did not, in the board's judgment, possess the qualifications to lead the district and was not moved forward in the search process. Yet, if it had happened that he was the most professionally qualified candidate, how would a board have reacted to the fact that the candidate was not forthcoming regarding the pending lawsuit? Would this or any other candidate have been eliminated because of an act of omission? Does a candidate have an obligation to inform a recruiter about a pending legal matter even if not asked on an application? What would have occurred if the candidate had been appointed and the court case turned out to be nasty and publicized? It is for these reasons that a recruiter must know if a candidate is involved in any legal proceedings.

It is important that a recruiter not automatically eliminate a candidate because of a legal issue. Being forthcoming with the facts can work to a candidate's advantage. For example, I worked with a candidate who had been arrested but later was appointed to a responsible position. At my suggestion, he informed the new employer about his arrest at the beginning of the search. His arrest was for a foolish, almost childish, act but one with substantial media coverage because of his public position.

Rather than remain silent on the matter, he was forthcoming with the new board during the interview stage. He was able to explain the circumstances that led to his arrest because he took the initiative. Had he not done so, the situation would have placed both the board and him on the defensive. The board understood what had happened and hired him in spite of the arrest on this minor charge. It remained a nonissue because of the candidate's openness. It helped that the candidate was outstanding at his work.

SEXUAL OR PHYSICAL MISCONDUCT

If a candidate has been involved in a sexual or physical misconduct matter, regardless of whether the person was arrested or convicted, it is a serious matter and is of concern to a consultant and employer. If the potential employer conducts thorough background checks in a candidate's current school district and community of residence, it will eventually discover this information. It is not unknown to have educators arrested and convicted on sexual abuse charges. As a recruiter, you need to have a process in place to uncover this type of information.

Physical abuse in education is less common, but it occurs. Again, this type of conduct has no place in education, and those in positions of responsibility need to be ever vigilant, taking great care before hiring those suspected of such conduct and terminating those who engage in it. Because both types of activity are criminal offenses, a background check that involves a fingerprint check with the FBI or the state police will most likely reveal this information. A responsible recruiter will also check with the State Department of Education in the present and former states in which the candidate worked to determine if her or his license to teach or administer has been revoked or if there is any action pending against her or him.

ALCOHOL ABUSE

Educators have been forced out of jobs because of alcohol abuse on school property. Often, those who abuse alcohol find themselves involved in automobile accidents or being stopped for erratic driving. When a public figure is arrested for driving while under the influence, it is news and it often leads to the person stepping down from a prominent position. We have witnessed many important public figures forced from their positions because of embarrassing events caused by alcohol abuse. Is there any doubt that teachers and administrators are public figures?

As a recruiter, you should consult with your attorney to understand what you as an employer are obligated to provide in the way of employee assistance. Alcohol abuse could form the basis for eliminating a candidate from contention. It is important to note that once employed, the district may be obligated to provide assistance to an employee with an alcohol-related problem. You should consult your attorney about whether the district needs a policy statement on hiring recovering alcoholics and drug addicts so that you adhere to the law.

EXTRAMARITAL AFFAIRS

During ten years as a consultant, I worked with two superintendent candidates who were involved in extramarital affairs at the time they applied for superintendent positions. Both the consultant and the potential employer did not have this information at the outset of the search. Interestingly enough, each was from a state that was at least one thousand miles from the districts in which he had applied for a position. Both affairs became known once the names of the superintendents were announced as semifinalists and the news reached their home communities.

An important point to be made is that if you, as the recruiter, have an applicant whose name becomes public before the time you complete background checks, you can be assured that the media will initiate an immediate background check on the candidate. More than likely, the media check will be more thorough than the one the district conducts! Members of the media are part of a special brotherhood and sisterhood wherein information is shared across all local and state boundaries. The same can be said for teacher associations. When you think about it, the National Education Association has what amounts to a branch office in practically every city, town, and hamlet in the United States. There is nothing in a candidate's professional past that even the smallest teacher association in the country cannot learn about through its network. Once a local teachers' association learns of a candidate's name, it activates its own national network. These initiatives by the media and teachers' associations can be particularly damaging when the candidate has applied for the position of superintendent of schools or building principal. The Internet has opened still more avenues to pursue background information about a candidate.

The lesson for the recruiter is that you must complete background checks before the media and the teacher and administrator associations conduct theirs! Of equal importance, you must validate your information with at least one other source.

These two extramarital cases were particularly serious because each male superintendent had an affair with the chairwoman of the board for which he worked. The publicity surrounding these two cases led to four careers being seriously damaged: the resignations of the two superintendents and two chairwomen.

NONRENEWAL AND TERMINATION OF SERVICES

Nonrenewal is a common activity, especially as it affects teachers who, for one reason or other, do not live up to district expectations. I stress to candidates that they must learn to turn down job offers if the chances of success in the district that offered a contract are minimal. Some districts do not possess the financial or human resources to provide the support new employees require. In other districts nonrenewal may be part of the culture.

Nonrenewal is also a common occurrence in districts that automatically nonrenew all nontenured teachers as a matter of practice pending a final district budget. In other cases, nonrenewal is used to reduce staff. As the potential employer, you need to determine the exact reason a candidate may have been nonrenewed. You must not rely on a single source for your information. There are those who will mislead you to move a nonperformer out of their district.

If the candidate was nonrenewed for reasons other than a routine district practice of nonrenewing all nontenured teachers or as a result of a legitimate reduction in force, you need to explore in detail the reason for the nonrenewal. Nevertheless, you need to carefully research a "reduction in force" nonrenewal since it may be a convenient way to remove a nonperformer. When I have an applicant who was nonrenewed, I request that she or he prepare a detailed narrative, giving as much information as possible, and then attach it to the application. The narrative serves three important purposes. First, it helps the candidate clarify what happened and to identify the events leading up to the decision. Second, it assists the candidate to avoid a repeat of the incidents that led to nonrenewal. Third, it provides the recruiter with sufficient information to begin to ask appropriate questions of the candidate. While the narrative is prepared from the perspective of the candidate, the accuracy of the statement speaks volumes about the candidate's professionalism and integrity.

If a candidate was nonrenewed or terminated for criminal, ethical, moral, or real or suspected illegal fiduciary reasons, he or she has a serious problem. In this case, the person needs to have professional and legal advice about what to do. As the potential employer, you need to take great care in making a decision about such a candidate. Clearly, the risk is high for the new employer.

A VOTE "NOT TO EXTEND"

Superintendents are often in a situation where, rather than being nonrenewed, they are subject to an action by the governing board that decides "not to extend" a contract. The distinction between *action for nonrenewal* and *board action not to extend* can be important depending on specific circumstances. Nonrenewal occurs most often when a superintendent is in the last year of a multiple-year contract and the governing board makes it clear that the current year is to be the last year and formalizes it, voting publicly not to renew the person's contract.

An action not to extend a contract usually occurs when a superintendent is operating under a multiple-year contract, and each year requests the board to extend it for another year. For example, take the case of a superintendent with a three-year contract. At the end of the first year, the superintendent requests that another year be added to the contract so that it remains three years in length. He usually requests this every year. Eventually, the governing board may either vote formally not to extend, or it may remain silent on the superintendent's request, which has the same effect as not extending the contract. However, a board's remaining silent is of benefit to the employee in most cases because the matter is kept out of the public arena. When this occurs, the superintendent has to determine why the board took the action it did. If it was over an issue or matter that can be resolved, the superintendent may stay on for another year or attempt to earn an extension. If he or she determines that the board would like the superintendent to leave, the superintendent usually begins a job hunt. It is not unusual for a board to decline to be specific as to why it did not want to extend a contract. In such a case, the superintendent is faced with a dilemma: stay or begin a search.

When a school district hires a consultant to work on a search, the consultant spends considerable time researching the events that led to a vote not to extend. This is where a consultant relies on her or his national network of professional associates and personal investigative skills to ferret out the details of the vote not to extend. Usually, consultants are outstanding at this activity. When a district conducts its own superintendent search, it usually does not possess the talent to get to the bottom of such a vote; therefore, it needs to employ tactics different from the ones used in hiring teachers and building-level administrators.

In the case of administrators, especially superintendents, being nonrenewed or terminated is not a professional tragedy if either occurred for the right reason. It happens to many of us. Recruiters must be careful in not rejecting, out of hand, those who fall into this category. Many administrators take positions that turn out to be something other than what they professed to be. Administrators are often caught between warring factions on the governing board or community leaders. Many times the nonrenewal or termination may have nothing to do with a candidate but rather with a secret board agenda that was not made known to the candidate upon hiring.

Once again, the recruiter should ask for a narrative that affords the candidate an opportunity to describe what happened. The recruiter must emphasize to the candidate the need to be accurate because the reader has to be convinced that the candidate was on the correct moral, professional, and ethical side of the issue that led to nonrenewal or termination.

I have used the device of the narrative many times and have found that those who believe they did nothing wrong complete the narrative. Others reject the idea of the narrative simply by not completing it. That itself speaks volumes.

I personally know of numerous cases where superintendents have been nonrenewed. In many instances, I have worked with these same superintendents as they sought new employment. Many, if not most, of them had earned the right to serve again. A few rightfully did not earn renewal. A handful should never have been in the educational field at all. Recruiters should not be quick to reject as candidates, teachers or administrators, those who may have had a one-time negative experience. This may have been due to factors beyond their control, such as a shift in partisan politics.

Lessons Learned

There are three lessons to be learned when recruiters think about nonrenewal, termination, and an action not to extend:

First, the reason for the action taken against a candidate is important to any district to which the candidate applies. As the recruiter, you need to discover the facts before making a judgment.

Second, if the action taken was for moral, ethical, or fiduciary failings that were proven, the recruiter must take special precautions before extending a contract of employment. If you employ a candidate with this type of record, you are at greater risk than the new employee!

Third, if nonrenewal was for a routine reduction in the workforce, a candidate should not be tainted by the nonrenewal action, and you should be interested in the candidate.

I want to emphasize the value of the narrative mentioned several times earlier. The narrative, if forthright, helps the candidates clarify their thoughts and set new courses for themselves. For the potential employer, it is a starting point for the interview. The length of the document depends on the issues and complexities involved. It is not intended that the narrative justify wrongdoing or improprieties on the part of a candidate; rather, it is for those who rightly believe they deserve second chances. Does not each of us deserve a second chance?

Not that you do not have enough reasons to worry about the recruiting process, chapter 9 discusses the issues surrounding the hiring of insiders and favorites.

⑨

INSIDERS AND FAVORITES

There are at least two types of appointments made to an open position that are disheartening to a qualified candidate who is not appointed to the position. The first is for a candidate to learn—whether by way of the grapevine, professional networking, or gossip—that an insider was appointed to the position, that the insider was the superintendent's or governing board's choice from the beginning, and that the interviewing process was used merely as legal cover. The second type of appointment that shakes the confidence of candidates is that of the outside favorite.

The "insider" label is employed in this section to identify anyone who is employed in a district but not necessarily in the same building or unit where the vacancy exists. An insider appointment usually occurs when the district has an employee who, although he or she may not be the best candidate, has considerable support from high-ranking administrators, particularly the superintendent or governing board members.

There are many reasons why an insider may be appointed to a position ahead of a more qualified candidate from outside the district. A new superintendent may use an insider appointment as a way to build instant popularity with others in the district by allowing local employees to become instant administrators without really earning the position. It may be used to pacify insiders who objected to the former superintendent's philosophy wherein all positions were widely advertised and which frequently resulted in positions being filled by more qualified candidates from outside the district. There are times when some governing board members think that a particular insider deserves the new position, someone who was especially helpful to a governing board member's children or who is popular with the student body. Then there is the case of someone who has been around for many years and has "earned" the position based on her or his long tenure. Occasionally, an insider is promoted to a new position primarily to be removed from a currently held position. Today there are more superintendents who are adjunct professors than ever before, as universities move away from the expense of maintaining tenured faculty. Consequently, there are times when an insider may be appointed because the superintendent is an adjunct professor in a university leadership program and promotes those in that university program who also happen to work for her or him. Insiders are occasionally appointed because they are part of an internal leadership-training program and are used as evidence that the program works.

There are other reasons why insider appointments are made, but whatever the reason for promoting an insider, it is always the wrong reason if the process is tainted. Appointing an insider based on any form of bias is no better than yielding to political or patronage pressure. A governing board that tolerates such a system is shirking its oversight responsibilities. A superintendent who promotes insider appointments to gain professional capital threatens the integrity of the entire recruiting process.

It remains a mystery to me how a superintendent can make an inside appointment without conducting a full-scale search that reaches as many potential candidates as possible. How does one build an outstanding system without outstanding personnel? A leader has no idea of the effectiveness of an internal leadership program unless insiders in the program go head-to-head with those from the outside and with others on the inside who feel locked out of the process. No matter how qualified a particular insider may be, there needs to be a competitive comparison with others. If, however, the search is already tainted by virtue of the insider's having the support of the internal staff, then no search should be conducted and a direct appointment should be made forthwith.

A superintendent's role in a search is similar to that of a search consultant in that the process for selection must be clean and transparent.

Anything less is unacceptable. During interviews for a consulting position, I have advised governing boards not to conduct a search if there is
a strong tendency to hire an insider. Such a search amounts to a sham
and brings discredit to the district and humiliation to the candidates
who apply from the outside. It also diminishes the reputation of the consultant. Applying and competing for a position is a stressful event; a candidate does not need the humiliation of uselessly competing for a job
that is already spoken for.

Assume, for the sake of argument, that the insider has no apparent
advantage in that no one encouraged her or him to apply and that
there is no particular reason why she or he should receive the appointment. In other words, there appears to be a level playing field.
The process is as it should be. However, the recruiter still needs to take
two precautions.

First, all inside candidates are to be informed that they will receive no
advantage simply because they are insiders. The only exception may be
a contractual one with the local teacher or administrative associations
wherein a governing board agreed with the associations to interview all
insiders regardless of qualifications.

Second, anyone whose hands touch the recruiting process in any way
must be informed that the playing field must remain level. For example,
it may happen that the insider may ask a clerk or friend in the personnel department how many applicants there are for the position. Inno-
cently, the clerk or friend may reveal this information and more, such as
the names of the other applicants. This is a violation of the ground rules
since no other candidate has access to the information.

Third, the interviewers in the process must be informed that an insider is to be given no advantage. This is not a case of giving credit for
military service. While it is true that an insider may have more information about the district than an outsider, it is no reason to think that it
makes the insider more qualified. If that were the case, there would be
no reason to ever go outside the district for candidates! In fact, I reject
this concept to the extent that when a new superintendent is hired in
one of my searches, I strongly recommend to the hiring board that the
outgoing superintendent leave on a Friday afternoon and the new superintendent arrive on the following Monday and that there be no over-
lap or uncomfortable transition!

If someone is sufficiently talented to be appointed superintendent, then he or she is talented enough to begin work without the assistance of the outgoing superintendent. In my mind this is true of all positions. Now, if a district is foolish enough to hire a new administrator who does not possess the talent and confidence to move directly into a position without assistance, then one should conclude that it was the wrong choice of a candidate. The point is that while an insider may have more local data, it does not make him or her any better qualified for the job. So often this is used as a way to justify an inside appointment.

The second type of appointment that threatens the integrity of the recruiting system and shakes the confidence of all candidates is that of the outside favorite. How does this work? It resembles the insider activity in that the superintendent or other influential administrators in the district encourage or nominate an individual employed in another district to apply for an opening. The candidate then applies believing that she or he is the favored candidate. In fact, when candidates apply through invitation, it is reasonable for them to believe that they are finalists for the positions. The higher the rank of the people soliciting the candidates, the more positive the candidates are in believing that the position is theirs. In some cases, there may be no advertising for the position, as a way to limit the number of applications.

The interesting thing about inviting an outsider to apply is that the insider who applies without invitation believes that the process will allow him or her to compete when, in fact, the position is essentially committed to an outsider. It reverses the discrimination that was explained in the insider job placement.

It is through recruiting that a district has the most effective opportunity to propel a district upward, to a status that places it among the best performing school systems in the nation. It follows that if the recruiting system is flawed in any way, the opportunity to improve a school system begins to slip away. Putting brakes on a system sliding downhill is far more difficult than pushing it uphill to excellence. Once a district acquires a reputation for not operating its recruiting system openly, it diminishes its ability to attract the best candidates.

Chapter 10 provides a suggested design of a perfect application, which yields the greatest number of qualified candidates.

⑩

A PERFECT APPLICATION

In addition to searching for school superintendents on behalf of governing boards, I also search for central office and building administrators. When on the latter type of assignment, I work for the superintendent rather than the governing board of the district. In most searches for central office administrators and building principals, I recommend that the superintendent allow me to design the application rather than use the district application. I use the district application with reluctance because most applications are too lengthy and request information that is not essential at the early stage of a search. In addition, a district application is usually generic in nature and not designed for a specific employee group.

A lengthy application is a burden to some candidates. It discourages many from applying. When a search is conducted during the summer, a recruiter needs to employ an abbreviated application to attract applicants who are concentrating on their vacation schedule and travel plans and have little time to complete lengthy forms or deal with lengthy application procedures. This is especially true of candidates who are highly qualified and who are being courted by several districts.

The easier the application process, the more likely candidates are to apply. Making the process simple helps you gain an edge over school systems competing for superior candidates. In rare cases, you may not want to use an application at all, relying solely on a cover letter and resume to attract candidates. A district needs to do what it must to gain an advantage over other districts that are also in the marketplace for outstanding candidates.

Much of the information requested on a lengthy application form can be obtained later in the process when the number of applicants has been reduced. For example, some districts require a writing sample. It is unnecessary to request all applicants to prepare a writing sample since it is not an important factor during an initial screening of applicants. Thus, the recruiter wastes the time of many applicants in this way and discourages others from applying. It is also wasteful of the recruiters' time if they are reading documents that have little or no relevance at the early stage of the process.

A word is necessary about the "writing sample." A recruiter uses it to assess the writing ability of a candidate and to better understand how a candidate thinks. Used in the context of this manuscript, the sample is an original writing on a topic selected by the recruiter. The actual writing usually takes place on-site under controlled conditions, although some recruiters allow the writing to take place off-site.

Most superintendent candidates do not prepare writing samples unless they are considered finalists. By refusing to submit a writing sample as a condition of the initial application process, they eliminate themselves as candidates; thus, they reduce the pool of potentially qualified candidates. The same condition holds true when recruiting busy central office and building-level administrators.

I suggest dealing with the writing sample issue by informing all candidates, at the time they apply, that a writing sample may be requested later in the search cycle. By informing them at the outset, you reserve the right not to require a writing sample, and you prevent a candidate from claiming that the district changed the conditions of the search once it was launched, should you decide to require a writing sample.

Most candidates provide the writing sample if they know they are rising to the top in the process. It is a more efficient use of the recruiter's time to request a writing sample only of those who are moving forward in the process. If a writing sample is required, my personal preference is that it be completed on-site so that the recruiter has confidence that the candidate wrote it. It is for this reason that I do not suggest that essay questions be included in the application.

What standards are used to assess the writing sample? In most cases there is no formal process. Rather, the samples are given to the interviewers who read them and make personal judgments. The sample is but one aspect of the interviewing process, and it is usually given whatever weight the interviewers decide on. If the content of the sample is interesting or controversial, interviewers can query the candidate on the topic.

There is an option to the writing sample requirement if a governing board or superintendent is adamant about having the candidates demonstrate literary proficiency. In some searches we ask that the candidate submit scholarly writings—that is, material that has been published in professional journals, in book form, or as a book chapter. A sidebar to this request is to have candidates who have not published professionally include copies of material they wrote and distributed within their school systems. Both are reasonable requests, but as a recruiter you have no assurance that the candidates actually authored the materials. This is unlike a writing sample that is prepared during the interview process, on-site, with the employer selecting the topic.

I strongly suggest that all applications be printed only on one side and be no longer than two pages. A one-sided application has the advantage of being easily reproduced in a high-speed copier. While this may appear to be a minor matter, it saves significant time when multiple copies are being produced for members of an interviewing committee.

An application of employment is only as good as the information it collects. The information collected is valuable only if it affords a recruiter the opportunity to make distinctions among candidates and conduct an early analysis of the quality of the applicants. Unfortunately, similar to many other details involved in the operation of a school system, the application form rarely undergoes a revision. Every recruiter should consider making revisions to the form at the end of every recruiting cycle. Revisions to the existing form should be based on information that was needed but not provided and collected but not needed.

As a consultant, I view the application from several perspectives, regardless of whether it is the formal, hard-copy application or an online version. For starters, I need basic biographical information about a candidate. "What's your name? Where do you live? What are the several methods available to contact you? Am I allowed to reach you at work? How do I contact you if you are on vacation?" A social security number may be requested if it is needed to check the status of an application with state agencies. These are not all of the questions that need to be asked, but they suffice to give the recruiter an idea of what is necessary. The recruiter is in the best position to assess whether an application is effective in collecting good biographical data.

Why are these data important? Whether I am working as a private consultant or as a recruiter for a school system, I need to make efficient use of my time, and in each instance wherein a candidate does not provide these basic data, I expend my time and energy to collect them. Since the candidate is the one seeking a position, she or he must do the work to provide information. I generally take the position that if I find it difficult to reach a candidate, I stop trying and move on to another qualified applicant. Recruiters should take the same tack since their time is also limited.

Without good biographical data, I am unable to initiate a preliminary background check, which always begins with a discussion with the candidate. If you are unable to reach the candidate, there can be no discussion. Clients pay me to perform my work, not that of the candidate. Recruiters are in the same position as a consultant in that their time is finite. Time spent with negligent candidates is time taken from cooperative candidates.

Each state has a different set of regulations that govern the contracts of employees, especially administrators. Some states provide continuing contracts to administrators who are tenured; therefore, it may not be important to ask questions relating to length of contract. In other states, employment of administrators is at the discretion of the superintendent who determines the conditions of employment and compensation.

If a recruiter is employed in a state where administrators are subject to annual voting by a governing board to extend contracts, then it is important to raise questions on the application that address contract matters. In the case of superintendents, they usually work on three- to six-year contracts. What questions should be asked of them? First, it is important to know the date that the most recent contract renewal vote was taken and the expiration date of the new contract. If a contract is expiring in the current year, then the governing board needs to understand why it is not being extended. If a candidate indicates that a contract has not been renewed or that there is a vote not to extend, the governing board has to determine why such a vote occurred. If there is any stage of a search where quality investigative skills are required, now is that time!

A superintendent should not be offered a contract of employment until all questions relating to his or her present and past positions have been fully answered. When a consultant is involved, there is a greater chance that employment issues are fully explored. If a governing board conducts the search, it may want to employ a consultant to handle the background-check portion of the search or to design the background-check process.

Once employment questions have been answered satisfactorily, the recruiter or governing board needs to determine the candidate's current compensation and what increases the candidate will receive if she or he remains in the current position for the following year. In my role as superintendent/recruiter, I always wanted to determine if the salary schedule in my district was sufficiently flexible to allow me to hire an outstanding administrator. My rule of thumb was that I wanted to provide a salary increase of at least 10 percent over her or his current salary if hired during a contract year or 10 percent over the salary she or he would receive in the next school year. The only way to accomplish this is to accurately determine the candidate's current salary and the salary for the following year.

All applications must make provision for the candidate to list professional experience and educational background. It is a standard section of an application. Of greater importance is the section on certification. It is essential that candidates list certification numbers or endorsements for the state in which they are applying. My experience is that out-of-state candidates usually do not posses certification in the state in which they are applying. In nine cases out of ten, they will note on the application something to the effect of "I hold certification in (fill in the blank) and there is reciprocity with my state of (fill in the blank again)." Rarely have candidates actually researched the certification issue. They assume that every state has reciprocity with all others. They find it far simpler to use the wording noted here.

My home state, Connecticut, has no automatic or permanent reciprocity with any other state! It may be similar elsewhere. To process an application that is not clear and specific about certification is mostly a waste of time. Again, the slick candidate wants to transfer the responsibility to research this matter to the recruiter!

Every application needs to request letters of reference and names of additional persons to be contacted. The following is paraphrased from reference information included in chapter 6 of *Job Hunting in Education*. The chapter was written as a guide to candidates, and it explains what is required of them in terms of reference letters and names of other references. The information is reformatted in this guide for the benefit of the recruiter. It is to the advantage of both a candidate and a recruiter that the reference section of the application be exact and that there be a clear distinction between "references" and "letters of reference." Candidates often collect the wrong references, and recruiters are sometimes not sufficiently clear in terms of what is acceptable. Chapter 7 of this guide provides examples of how four out of six finalists for the position of superintendent of schools failed to provide what was requested in the way of reference information.

UNAVAILABLE INFORMATION

If for any reason candidates are unable to provide what is being requested, the recruiter should ask that the applicants write a note explaining why they cannot comply at this time and when, if ever, they can do so. The note should be attached to the application. For example, the district may request a letter of recommendation from a candidate's immediate supervisor, who may be out of the country for several weeks and unable to provide such a letter. If that situation occurs, then the recruiter is in a position to request a recommendation from another person or wait a short time for the supervisor to return.

LETTERS OF REFERENCE AND NAMES OF REFERENCES

Every district should request that letters of reference be attached to the candidate's application. The request for letters of reference often creates a dilemma for both the applicant and the employer. In the case of our firm, we require three current letters from professionals who know the candidate's work. In addition, we have a section that requires the applicant to list the names, current addresses, and phone numbers of three additional professional references. Please note that "letters of reference" are distinct from "names of references." In the first case, actual letters are attached to the application. In the latter case, the recruiter wants the names of three additional persons that can be contacted. The persons offered as references must be different from those persons who submitted letters of reference.

We also note on the application that if for any reason a candidate is unable to comply fully with the reference request, all that is required of the candidate is a phone call to inform us why the request cannot be met. For example, a superintendent applying for a new position is usually reluctant to ask a current employer for a reference at the beginning of a search because it could compromise the candidate in his or her own district. In the case of a superintendent, the most important reference is usually the chairperson of the governing board. Thus, it is understandable that initially there may not be full compliance with the letters-of-reference section. Whenever a candidate is not in full compliance with the reference requirement, the recruiter must be aggressive in following up with the candidate to complete this task.

A recruiter should expect that all letters of reference be dated. The most valuable are usually those that are current. An early warning sign to a recruiter that things may not be going well for a candidate is when she or he overwhelms you with numerous letters of reference, especially old, undated letters and letters from subordinates rather than supervisors.

Whoever in the district is assigned the responsibility to read and assess letters of reference must be skilled at reading between the lines and being sensitive to what has not been said. I find that some candidates include letters that they believe are helpful but that are interpreted otherwise by the consultant. Candidates tend to believe that when letters of reference are written on their behalf by noted educators, professors, or administrators, that this fact automatically implies that such letters are well written or that they make a positive statement about the candidates' work. This is not always true.

The following is an actual case involving a candidate for a central office position in my former district and his three letters of reference. As members of my staff were reading them, one employee noted that, although different administrators in the candidate's district appeared to have written the letters, there was a similar tone, vocabulary, syntax, and sentence structure to all of them and a consistent use of the same grammatical structure. When the letters were more closely examined, it became apparent that all three were printed on the same machine. Further compounding this issue was the fact that the candidate had used school system letterhead for all three letters.

To receive one letter on district letterhead is common practice, but to receive three letters from three different administrators written on the superintendent's letterhead was cause for concern. One of the three letters was from the candidate's superintendent, an educator with whom I had no earlier contact although we lived in the same state. I called the superintendent and asked if he had written the letter. He knew nothing of it. Checks with the other two references revealed that the candidate had written all three letters himself. In spite of his efforts, he could not disguise his writing style sufficiently to pull off this fraud. His candidacy, needless to say, went no further.

References Not to Be Contacted

Every application should require the names and phone numbers of additional references who can be contacted. These are individuals who have not submitted letters of reference for the candidate. Those who submit letters of reference usually know the candidate is seeking new employment. However, individuals who have not written letters and who are listed as additional references often do not know the candidate is in the job market. A candidate may list them but does not want them to be contacted unless he or she moves to the top in the process. If the candidate requests that you not contact references at this stage in the job search, the request should be honored, but the candidate needs to understand that at some point in the search all references (or as many as needed) will be contacted.

Appropriate References

Who are important references to the recruiting committee? The simple answer is only those persons who can speak with authority about the work of the applicant. All other references are superfluous. The recruiter must ignore the extraneous references. Individuals writing reference letters need to be clear about their relationships with the candidate and be in a position to know the details of the applicant's qualifications for the position. The letters should express context, time periods, and sound knowledge of the candidate. Therefore, the most important references to the recruiter are immediate supervisors or, in the case of a school superintendent, the chairperson of the board, then previous supervisors, followed by other professionals who are familiar with the candidate's work.

The least important references are those from subordinates and professionals the candidate evaluates, clergy, politicians, and parents. Using peers as references is appropriate only if they have worked closely with the candidate on specific projects. Such references, however, often carry minimal weight in the assessment of the candidate. The use of students and parents as references is appropriate for teachers since parents constitute their primary constituency. Nevertheless, some level of caution is suggested since those who have had a positive experience with the candidate generally write positive letters.

Once a district has letters of reference and the names of others to contact on behalf of a candidate, it is time to speak with all of them. There are always questions about the written references that need follow-up. As I experienced in the military, one compelling reason to contact references listed is to collect from them the names of other persons who may know of the candidate and who were not initially listed as references. How far you want to expand the list depends on the importance of the position being filled and the degree to which you may or may not be satisfied with what you hear from your first contacts.

Once you are satisfied that the list is complete, it remains for the investigator to raise questions that elicit the information needed to make the next decisions, such as to interview, to place someone in the finalist group, or to hire or not hire a candidate. As superintendent, I used a memo-type form that the appropriate employee used during the standard telephone reference-check procedure.

The following categories were utilized to ask questions of references. These data are what were required to make a decision to whether a teacher would be hired, but the topics are easily modified for administrative candidates.

Date of the call

Person contacted

Topics to be assessed: Command of subject, understanding of children, ambition, appearance, ability to manage students, ability to
relate to students, clarity of verbal expression, and professional maturity

Candidate's strongest asset

Candidate's weakest area

Determine if candidate was released from a contract

Determine if candidate was refused contract renewal

Recommendation to the superintendent to hire, not hire, other (explain)

Sign and date the form and submit to superintendent.

A separate form was required for each candidate. These forms were
kept on file as a way to review what went wrong if the candidate was not
successful. It allowed the superintendent to judge the effectiveness of
the employee who conducted the telephone background check and the
integrity of the responding school system.

At some stage in the recruiting process, it is necessary to conduct a
site visit to the candidate's home district, which is the subject of chapter
11, "Why Take a Trip?"

WHY TAKE A TRIP?

Throughout this guide, the case has been made that a school system is only as good as its employees. Every effort must be made to hire only the most competent persons, leaving the marginal candidates for other districts to employ. One of the most essential steps in the hiring process is the site visit. While every finalist for a superintendent's position must have a site visit conducted in his or her home community (and, often, in the previous one), it is not always clear if a site visit should be conducted for other administrators or teachers.

As a long-tenured superintendent, I have operated on the philosophy that under no circumstances is an administrator to be hired in my district unless a site visit is made to her or his district. An exception is when there is only one finalist who is from within the district, although in a large urban district an internal site visit may still be justified.

Up to this point in the hiring process, all references for the finalists have been through letters the candidate requested or through telephone checks. There has been no personal contact. Nothing substitutes, in my opinion, for a one-on-one discussion, on-site, with those who best know a candidate. However, many districts and some consultants have little use or time for site visits. Their objections can be classified as follows:

Objection 1: A site visit is financially costly since it means transport-ing several employees or governing board members to another site, which often means incurring transportation, lodging, and meal expenses.

My response: The financial cost of conducting a site visit pales beside the cost of terminating a mistake!

Objection 2: A site visit is costly in terms of time and energy to plan and execute the trip.

My response: Once a recruiter has developed a template for a typical site visit, the rest are relatively easy to plan and execute. Except in the case of a superintendent search, most of the team members are district employees for whom coverage is easily arranged. In the case of a superintendent search, most of the team comprises members of the governing board. My experience is that many members are in a position to arrange for time off to be on the visiting team.

Objection 3: A site visit is not worthwhile, because the candidates stack the meetings to their advantage.

My response: This is the most common reason for a district not to conduct a site visit, and it demonstrates the simplistic view a recruiter or governing board may have about how to get at the truth about a candidate. If I learned nothing else in my previous academic administrative work, it is that it makes little difference to whom you speak in terms of getting all the information you want. I have often used the following comment to explain my position: "Even your mother will tell tales about you if questions are asked in the right way, in the right context, in the right sequence, and by a skilled questioner." (This was axiomatic in military intelligence work.) It is for this reason that members of the site visit team must be chosen with care.

While this manuscript was being prepared, I was conducting a search for a governing board, the chair of which was a lawyer. When I suggested that he be a member of the site team, he responded with "I'm not a trial lawyer and do not possess good investigative skills." Although he acknowledged one of his shortcomings, it was also his way of saying, "Send someone who is capable of gathering vital information."

PURPOSE OF A SITE VISIT

A site visit is designed to validate a candidate's qualifications. You are on a mission to validate what interviewers observed or learned during all of the initial steps in the recruiting process, including a paper review of credentials, several interviews, and a preliminary background check. While the visit is designed to measure the candidates against the full array of duties for which they will be responsible in your district, you must also place emphasis on those specific qualifications that you identified during the interview process or that may have surfaced during focus sessions. If, for example, the district places significance on improving test scores for average students, then the visiting team needs to determine if the candidates have been successful in accomplishing this in their districts or are likely to be able to do so in the future. The site team needs to see hard data and speak with those in the district who can validate the candidates' claims of success.

WHO MAKES THE ARRANGEMENTS?

When the district is in charge of the site visit, either the superintendent of schools or the director of human resources organizes the site visit with the candidate. The district makes the decision about which school and lay communities the site team will meet, and the candidate handles the logistics of scheduling the meetings. If this is a superintendent search, the consultant acts in lieu of the superintendent, unless it is the governing board that is conducting the search, in which case its chair would be in charge of arrangements.

WHO ARE THE MEMBERS OF THE VISITING TEAM?

Who travels as a member of the site visit team is as critical as what it is each accomplishes upon arrival. First, you need a balance on the team, that is, members who represent the various constituents who will interact with the administrator. The members must be inquisitive and pleasant. They must enjoy the opportunity to meet new people and gather useful information. The underlying concern for the recruiter must be that members appointed to a site team are of the disposition to inquire, to ask questions, and to do what is necessary to validate what you have been led to believe is true about the candidate.

WITH WHOM DOES THE TEAM MEET?

This is always the most controversial area and one that critics most often put forth to discredit site visits. If the visit is not properly structured, then criticism is warranted. Properly constructed, it can accomplish its mission with success and with site team members enjoying themselves. The team, if the visit is successful, also becomes an important future support system for the new administrator. The site visit schedule includes the titles and names of those to be interviewed, the sequence of the meetings, and the length of meetings. When planning a visit, I schedule a fifteen-minute opening session with the candidate to review the schedule and a twenty-minute wrap-up session with the candidate to bring closure to the day. In between are scheduled the many other important meetings.

In preparation for a site visit, I provide the governing board or superintendent with a comprehensive list of possible contacts in a district. It is far more extensive than is needed, but it is designed to remind them that there are many groups that they often do not think about, such as taxpayer organizations, minority representative groups, social agencies in the community, the recreation department, the police department, and the historical society. Each community has active agencies and organizations that interact with the schools. The extensive list allows governing board members to select appropriate groups in the candidate's community with which to meet. The governing board members are requested to identify those individuals or groups on the list, by title, with whom they wish to meet. I then request the candidate to indicate individuals and groups with whom he or she wishes us to meet. Then I offer my suggestions based on many years of conducting site visits. At some point, we reach a consensus, and a schedule is developed.

I construct a schedule that allows a team to begin meetings by 9 AM and conclude by 3 PM. The following are the times usually allotted:

Individual meetings: fifteen minutes, except for meetings with major
   players
Meetings of three or more participants: thirty minutes
Meetings with groups of four or more: forty-five minutes
Meetings with large groups: forty-five minutes to one hour

The visiting team is divided into two groups, allowing it to conduct two meetings simultaneously.

QUESTIONS TO ASK

Questions are generally constructed as a result of earlier interviews, when certain topics were pursued and are of interest to the hiring district. Questions are also constructed from interviewers' expressed doubts about the candidate or from answers that need clarification. The most important questions are those that deal with the candidate's ability to work effectively with staff and those that assist the team to validate accomplishments that the candidate has described. The team needs to agree on most of the questions beforehand, recognizing that new questions emerge as the meetings progress. It is important for team members to be outstanding listeners to detect the slightest variation in opinions expressed. Good interviewers use what they learn from one group to raise questions with other groups.

Site visit members should ask any questions that they believe are important to make an accurate assessment of the candidate's work and qualifications. Many of the questions asked during the previous interviews can be reformatted and asked again as a way to compare the candidate's response to issues with the perceptions of his or her constituents. Site visit members should identify, from the list used during the preliminary interviews, those questions whose answers need clarification. Certainly, you need to ask questions that speak directly to answering what the district needs in its next leader.

How do members avoid being compromised? First, they should never assume that they are hearing the whole truth until the team breaks for lunch, at which time team members need to compare notes and decide if there is a need to change tactics in the afternoon sessions. Let me provide an example of where a team changed directions over lunch because of what they perceived as exaggerated statements made by staff members and the candidate.

The candidate stated at her several interviews that she knew most of the students in the three schools in her district: an elementary school, a middle school, and a high school. The morning meetings of the site visit team confirmed, from statements from some staff members, that this was probably so, but to the visiting team it appeared too good to be true. It seemed to be an expansion of facts. At lunchtime, the team divided itself into two teams. The first would continue with the afternoon meetings as scheduled, but the other had something else in mind! The team's plan rested on the fact that the superintendent, at the opening briefing in the morning, indicated she would be available all day if needed.

The second team called and asked if she would accompany the team on short visits to the three schools after lunch, never telling her what they had in mind. She agreed and escorted them through the three schools. No sooner had they entered the first building than students began to call out to her by her title with a sincere show of warmth and familiarity. They waved and otherwise sought her attention, and she responded to almost all of them by first name!

The same situation developed at the other two schools. It was evident that this superintendent had spent many hours in each school and knew the students and staff by first name. Did she know every student by first name? No, but she demonstrated a quality that the site team valued; she was a student's superintendent! Did she know every teacher they met by first name? She did. The team reported its findings to the full governing board. Later, she was appointed superintendent. It is not very often that the careful, daily incremental work as an administrator builds to such a glorious crescendo as happened in this case.

Still, another site visit worked to the disadvantage of the candidate. I led the team on the site visit in my role as consultant. The candidate had many good qualities and had two excellent interviews in the district. The governing board was not of one mind, so the results of the site visit could be decisive. Arrangements for the trip were made, and several important sessions in the candidate's district were scheduled, including meetings with the editor of the largest newspaper that covered his district and with the program director of the major television network. These were in addition to scheduled meetings with his governing board members and others in the schools and community.

The members of the visiting team were not experienced search committee members and needed reassurance throughout the site visit. Because of their passive role, I was required to take the initiative at all of the interviews. While much of what I heard was positive, there were subtle differences among the stories. Perhaps it was the sixth sense of being a longtime superintendent or just good training, but I felt the presence of an unpleasant undercurrent, the source of which I could not discern.

The first day ended with a dinner meeting with some, but not all, governing board members and their spouses attending. The dinner took place while we cruised the inland waterway on a large private yacht. The vessel belonged to the chairman of the governing board, or his nationally known corporation. There was an abundance of camaraderie, food, drink, and casual conversation.

It was only after the skipper was returning to his dock that I realized that this was essentially one big con game. The candidate was distracting us to avoid questioning. This point was driven home when he announced that he would be leaving us for a business trip immediately upon docking. This, of course, would allow no time for us to meet privately. He never intended to engage in a one-on-one conversation with the visiting team. While the cruise was delightful on a warm early summer evening and although the food and drink were excellent, there was no serious questioning of the chair or board members. My team, unsophisticated in some matters, was having a wonderful time on the ship. One member, however, had street smarts, and he realized the next day that he and I were on the same page.

The next morning when we convened, before our meeting with the candidate, we had a team that was divided in its assessment of the candidate. One board member (I had no vote, being the consultant) thought the search should be aborted, and three recommended it be continued. It was continued, but when the candidate's name was announced in the hiring district as being the finalist, the bottom fell out: the newspaper and local talk show hammered on the governing board until it called off the search. It is appropriate to say that all hell broke loose!

The specific issues that destroyed this search are neither appropriate nor useful to itemize. It is sufficient to say that this candidate was not the right choice for the job in spite of being a decent person. However, he had displayed exceptionally poor judgment in making two decisions in his current district that caused him irreparable professional harm. One decision had to do with an inappropriate placement on a salary schedule for a family member, and the other was an inappropriate fiscal decision. The lesson is that the governing board of the hiring district should have respected the single dissenting voice of one of its members, heeded the concern of the consultant, and called an immediate halt to the search to reconsider its next step. Its decision to proceed only delayed its admission of defeat and the need to shut down the search.

After the crisis passed, we restarted the search, and several months later the governing board hired a new superintendent, someone who is very successful today.

QUESTIONS OF MORALITY

Morality is always a major issue in the hiring of a new person. Adversaries may forgive professional inconsistencies, but they are not forgiving of moral failures, nor for that matter are the candidate's advocates. The disclosure of a moral turpitude issue quickly destroys a candidate and brings into question the ability of the recruiter and the governing board to conduct a search. Uncovering such an issue, if one exists, is difficult because a candidate usually makes every effort to keep it well hidden.

In dealing with this issue, you need to be discreet since raising a question in this arena may cause something of a negative nature to be created where nothing exists. However, as a member of a visiting committee, one can ask questions such as "Tell us what you know about this person's family relationships" or "Please give us a sense of the kind of person we are dealing with relative to his personal life" or "Is there anything in her background that you are aware of or have heard of that would make her unsuitable for a position of public trust?"

HISTORICAL PERSPECTIVE

In making a judgment about a candidate, the site visit team must not base it solely on the candidate's most recent experiences in the district. A longitudinal analysis would present a far more accurate portrait of the person. Everyone, whether a superintendent or CEO, in a decision-making position and who is devoted to policy change makes mistakes and has adversaries. The team must examine newspaper articles written over an extended period and not rely on the writings of a single reporter who, for whatever reason, may have an ax to grind against a person in a leadership position. What the team needs instead is a sense of a person's consistency, stability, effort, and quality of service. Do not rely on the perspective of one reporter or one television report since life in a leadership role is more comprehensive and complex than what is written in an epitaph.

ASSESSING A SITE VISIT

It is difficult to assess accurately your site visit results unless you had established, before the visit, specific areas you wanted to validate. If improvement in the quality of classroom instruction is the area of greatest importance, then you must be certain to raise those issues with all of the groups with whom you meet. If your concern is the need to improve school–community relations and personnel relations, then you must agree ahead of time that you will raise questions relative to these issues. Then, before you draw any conclusions following your site visit, you must meet as a group and share findings and impressions, being very specific about what you believe you heard or validated. Returning to your home district with "feelings" or "concerns" is not sufficient. The team, in reporting to the full governing board, must provide hard evidence that the candidate is the person of choice based on validated prior experience.

You must have overwhelming evidence that the candidate's experiences are such that she or he will be an outstanding superintendent in your community and will attain the goals shared with the governing board. Above all, the team cannot let good feelings mislead its members. You are cast in the role of an investigator, and like it or not, you must act like one! Assessments must be based on hard data. Soft data may provide you with a hint about potential and competence, but hard data are conclusive.

USE OF AN OUTSIDER ON SITE VISITS

When a site visit is conducted to validate the quality of service of potential hires below the rank of superintendent, the visit in most cases is under the direction of the superintendent or a person of his or her choosing. Superintendents have a good sense of the questions to be raised and the areas to investigate, particularly when conducting background checks on teachers and administrators. They are excellent at decoding the language of other educators.

When the site visit is conducted to check on the qualifications of a candidate applying for a superintendent's position, the visit is under the control of the governing board. In this case, it is best that the board employ a consultant to organize the site visit even if the consultant does not personally participate.

If funds are available, the board is well advised to include the consultant as a member of the site visit team. Consultants are usually former superintendents and have experience in interviewing and assessing. It is money well spent. Under no circumstances should the sitting superintendent be involved in any aspect of a replacement search, including the site visit!

HOW VALID IS THE INFORMATION
COLLECTED ON A SITE VISIT?

Superintendents and building administrators operate under public scrutiny and in the public arena. As a result, there is a tendency for their blemishes to be overblown and their successes to be underestimated or unappreciated. Successes are often not known.

The demands of their positions require them to make decisions that are not always well received. Employees, particularly in communities where there is a strong union presence, may not think highly of any district administrators. As a result, site visits to validate the credentials of superintendents and principals usually reveal some level of controversy. There is nothing necessarily negative about controversy as long as it relates to professional differences of opinion on educational matters. A site visit team must not be misled by a negative position taken by a teachers' association or a particular segment of the parent population. The task of the site visit team is to determine why there was controversy.

Activities viewed as negative by members of the superintendent's and principal's constituents may be seen as positive by a governing board. For example, teachers may be upset with a principal because of her or his aggressive and professionally demanding evaluations, while a superintendent may be looking for just such a principal for his or her district. During a site visit, a superintendent candidate may be judged by the teacher's association as setting the academic bar too high, while the hiring board and parents seek a superintendent who can bring academic rigor to a system. Judging what is positive or negative in a search is a matter of relative perspective.

A site visit is as important as the visiting team makes it. In the final analysis, the characteristics the team are trying to identify are those that one would look for in any educational leader: love of the work, commitment to the district or building, solid moral character, history of taking ethical positions on controversial professional matters, understanding the nuances of teaching and learning, and being committed to improving the lives of children and young adults. Your job as a member of the district's site visit team is to determine if the person you are assessing is the right person to work effectively with the constituents in your schools and community.

This chapter addresses the purpose and organization of a site visit, but long before the site visit occurs, decisions are made in the recruiting process about which candidates would make it through the very first stage of a search, the subject of chapter 12, "Many Apply, Few Are Chosen."

⑫

MANY APPLY, FEW ARE CHOSEN

Every school system faces at least one similar problem as it pertains to the recruiting process: how are the hundreds, if not thousands, of applications sorted as the first step in the selection process? Assuming for the moment and for purposes of illustration that the process has eliminated any outside political pressures, that patronage does not apply, and that the selection is left entirely to the district recruiter, what is the first step to be taken with the applications?

In chapter 1, "I Guarantee," I make a point that internal interests of a personal nature often enter into the selection process. It is not unusual for personnel who make the initial decision about which candidates move forward to favor candidates whom they know or know something about. In many instances, there are applications from substitute teachers in the district seeking full-time employment and paraprofessionals who recently received certification as a teacher, as well as from friends and acquaintances. While there is no certain way to eliminate favoritism, a recruiter can take steps to reduce it significantly. The following is one way, but certainly not the only way.

When I first started to advertise positions in my role as superintendent, I would simply indicate that there was an opening for a "fifth-grade teacher" or a "high school chemistry teacher," or a "special education

teacher for the elementary grades." When necessary, the ad would include more specific language, such as "high school chemistry teacher
with a minor in biology." Personnel engaged in the initial screening of
applications used the wording in the ad as the basis for their initial
screening. With the language being so general, it was easy enough to
move forward in the process with a variety of candidates, including
friends and favorites.

Why is this of concern? The two most important steps in the recruiting process are the first and final steps, with the first step being putting
an application into play and the final step being the position's formal appointment. However, without making the first cut there is no other step
for the candidate! It is for this reason that extreme care must be taken
when applications are first selected for further consideration.

Having some suspicion that the selection process was not entirely on
a level playing field, I instituted a hiring criteria form that then served
as the basis for the creation of the ad and as a guide for those responsible for the initial screening of applications. Listed in the following is the
content of the form used for teacher candidates. A separate form with
different criteria was utilized for administrative positions. The contents
of the form are displayed for illustrative purposes only, since each recruiter will have to design one that is district appropriate. Nevertheless,
whatever the content, it must first focus on neutralizing both inside and
outside favoritism.

THE FORM

Teaching position to be filled (be specific as to grade, subject, special
considerations, school, and specific expectations)
Anticipated starting date
Quality of academic preparation required (list grade point average or
other marking criteria, e.g., top 25 percent of the class)
Level of academic preparation required (i.e., BA, MA, sixth year,
PhD/EdD)
Required experience (be specific about grade or level and years of ex-
perience)

Diversity of experience required (e.g., experience working with non-English-speaking students in a suburban setting)

Primary certification required (elementary level through sixth grade)

Secondary certifications required or desired (e.g., middle school English)

Special or unusual department or grade-level needs (e.g., proven ability to assume leadership role)

Optional criteria (e.g., willingness to assume paid after-school activities)

The form was completed by the subject supervisor, building principal, or central office employee, depending on the administrative structure. Regardless of who completed the form, it required the written approval of the principal and an appropriate central office administrator.

While one may debate the criteria sought in the successful candidate, the fact is that the form reduced the number of unqualified candidates moved forward. If a candidate met all of the criteria, then she or he was moved forward in the process. At any stage, the district could forgo or replace, with the approval of the superintendent, any of the criteria, but it would take a strong argument for this to occur. When it did occur, the reason was that few or none of the candidates met the criteria, for example. There should be a natural resistance about eliminating agreed-on criteria. Once this starts to happen, the process itself begins to degenerate.

This process assumes that the first decisions are made at the department or building level, which is the most common way to decide such things in small- or medium-sized districts. In urban, large suburban, or county districts, the hiring is most likely done at the central office level. This, in my mind, is the most ineffective way to build strong and unified faculties and departments. Nevertheless, it may be the only way for a large organization to operate. Since the majority of school systems in the nation are classified as small, the selection process should be building or department based.

Whenever a district attempts to improve on what it does, it should not rely solely on what others do. It is true that much can be learned from the successes of other systems or from the advice offered in guides such

as this one, but all efforts to improve the process must be tailored to local needs and conditions. The saying "All roads lead to Rome" is good
advice when a district seeks new pathways to improvement. What must
not be compromised when local needs or conditions are considered is
the ethical underpinning of your effort. A district's hiring criteria may
differ from others, but the primary reason for utilizing specifically tailored recruiting criteria remains the same: promoting only those candidates who are superior in talent, experience, and potential for growth.
School systems do not plummet to mediocrity; they slide into it in small
yet discernable increments. Everything possible must be done to avoid
your system's slipping into an abyss.

Once a candidate moves beyond the initial screening stage, the personal aspect of the search begins. At some point in the process he or she
meets the interviewers, which relates to the content of chapter 13, "Who
Are the Interrogators?"

⓭

WHO ARE THE INTERROGATORS?

In chapter 6, I emphasize that there is a need to utilize interviewers who are qualified to judge subordinates, peers, and superiors. I make the case that not all interviewers are born equal and the degree to which they are incapable of accurately judging others is the degree to which a qualified candidate may be overlooked and a marginal one promoted or hired. Group interviewing has become the norm in most school systems, primarily to develop a collaborative culture; but group interviewing also has the advantage of minimizing the impact of a marginal interviewer. A problem arises when the entire group has had minimal training or no interview training; consequently, some members are not qualified to make appropriate judgments about specific candidates. Nevertheless, there is security, if not strength and competency, in numbers.

When a candidate appears before an interviewing committee, he or she would like to inquire of the committee members, "Please, who is asking the question?" When the first question is put forth, the candidate would like to know if this person has an agenda and, if so, what is it?

A candidate cannot help but wonder what group the person raising the question represents: teachers, administrators, parents, or community? All are possibilities. The candidate understands that each interviewer comes to the table from a different perspective, perhaps with a different end game in mind. Knowing who and how each interviewer operates is valuable information. Understanding the makeup of the committee, how it was formed, what prejudices members may hold, the diversity of views it possesses, and the mission it was given become essential data for the candidate. The recruiter must format the group interview with the following factors in mind.

The candidate needs to know before the interview whether it will be person-to-person or conducted in a group setting.

The candidate needs to know, before the first question is posed, who is at the table and what group each person represents.

A name card, clearly printed and large enough to be read from the candidate's position at the table, needs to be positioned in front of each interviewer.

The chair of the interviewing committee has the responsibility to introduce the candidate to each member of the committee, and the committee members in turn must introduce themselves to the candidate.

Once the introductions are completed, the chair must explain to the candidate and to the interviewers how the meeting will unfold: length of time for the interview, the approximate number of questions to be asked, whether there will be time at the end for the candidate to ask questions (hopefully none) or to provide a closing statement (highly preferable), the next steps in the recruiting process, and a suggested time frame for those steps to occur.

If the name cards have both first and last names, indicate to the candidate that first names are the preferable form of address.

The chair arranges for one of the interviewers to ask the first question so that the interview has a smooth beginning.

All of the interviewers possess the candidate's cover letter, application, and resume. They should not have any written references or transcripts at this time, to avoid prejudicing this screening interview.

The chair has conducted a briefing session for the interviewers so that they understand the need to adhere to sound interviewing protocols, avoid questions that are prohibited by law, behave professionally, and otherwise be provided with detailed information on how to conduct an interview.

The setting for the interview must be a pleasant one with chairs and tables arranged so that everyone has eye contact with the candidate and so that the candidate, in turn, has a clear view of the interviewers. All tables should be equipped with vanity skirts.

Finally, all interviewers refrain from passing notes, whispering to other interviewers, and bringing food to the table.

The aforementioned suggestions are only a partial list of the factors that need to be considered if an interview is to be effective. A consultant is helpful in attending to the details that make for a perfect interview and interview setting. The goal is to have a perfect setting, but one needs to be prepared to deal with absences, time crunches, schedule conflicts, lost resumes, disturbed interviewers, and more!

The chair must be fully qualified to brief members on effective interviewing techniques. Unfortunately, most chairs are actually not qualified to do so, especially on those matters that have legal ramifications. If the chair is not fully capable, then the human relations department needs to engage the services of someone in the district with more appropriate experience, or it needs to bring in an outside expert. It is wasteful of human resources to bring interviewers together when they are not well qualified or properly trained.

The recruiter needs to make a careful assessment of the makeup of the interviewing committee. Although many may express a desire to serve, only a few are capable of serving. Unless a committee member is willing to make herself or himself available for all of the interviews scheduled for the current round and is willing to participate in a training session, that person should not be selected.

INTERVIEWING COMMITTEES IN GENERAL

Understanding who is sitting on an interview committee is important to the candidate since she or he needs to tailor responses to different audiences. This does not mean she or he will play to an audience, but it does require providing information that each member seeks. The most difficult committee for a candidate to deal with is a mixed committee, a committee comprising far too many constituencies in the system (parents, unions, administrators, governing board members, and support staff, to name a few). The difficulty arises because each member is often waiting for a response that others do not seek. This is compounded by the fact that in education, unlike most other professions, interviewing committees often include individuals from outside the profession.

For example, a committee interviewing a superintendent candidate usually has representatives from civic organizations, political entities, town employees, parent groups, minority organizations, senior citizens groups, and others. Consider the potential conflict for the candidate when parents want greater expenditures for education while representatives from any one of the other groups may be seeking a cap on the tax rate. Principals may desire a strong leader while a governing board may want someone who can be micromanaged. What is a candidate to do? If she or he knows who is on the committee, she or he can answer the question truthfully for the person who asked it and then explain to other members why this may be in conflict with their thoughts.

Even within the professional staff, there are potential conflicts. For example, teachers and parents may not agree on student grouping practices or on how teacher planning time should be utilized. Parents may seek a principal who is able to "clean house" while the staff likes things as they are. Candidates need to speak honestly and frankly and should not play to any one member.

INTERVIEWING COMMITTEES ORGANIZED BY POSITION

There was a time in the distant past when principals hired teachers, superintendents hired administrators, and governing boards hired superintendents. This was accomplished without the inclusion of other parties. Over the past twenty-five years or so there has been a steady change in the hiring process such that a committee with a diverse membership fills almost every position. While the administrator in charge of a search may favor one candidate over another, it is difficult not to follow the recommendation of the interviewing committee. An administrator who ignores such a recommendation often does so at his or her own peril. Because of the immense leverage a committee has, a candidate must understand the makeup of the committee and know how to deal with the diverse membership.

Teacher Interviewing Committees

If you are interviewing a teacher candidate, your committee should comprise the building administrator or department chair, other teachers from the same grades or department, and parents. It is helpful for the diversity of a committee to include a nonclassroom staff member, such as a guidance counselor or social worker. In smaller districts, a central office person is sometimes included.

If a candidate has advanced to this stage, it means that her or his application and other materials were reviewed at the building or department level. In some situations it is possible that she or he had a screening interview before the committee interview. Because of the preliminary review, you determine that the candidate appears qualified and should be treated as such. If you find her to be qualified, then you can assume that other districts arrived at the same conclusion. You must not lose the candidate because of procedural errors or human missteps. Accept him or her as an equal from then on.

As innocent as your committee makeup may appear to the candidate, it represents many competing interests. The teachers on the committee are usually the most outspoken ones in the school. That, generally speaking, may be how they got to serve! They may want a pliable recruit while the principal may want a strong individual. The grade level to which the candidate would be assigned may have had low test scores for several years, and the superintendent may want to hire a teacher who can bring academic rigor while the other grade-level teachers may be content with things as they are.

The point is that an innocuous-looking committee always has diverse opinions about what is sought in the new staff member. Do not expect the candidate to express the "right" answers for all of the committee members. It is just not possible. What you should be interested in is whether the candidate is supportive of the correct moral and ethical side of those issues that best serve students. In the final analysis, the students are the candidate's primary constituency, not the members of the interviewing committee!

Administrator Interviewing Committees

Because of the range of administrative positions in a district, the composition of interviewing committees varies. However, there are similar components to all of them. The district should include representatives from the respective administrative, teacher, and parent organizations and from the central office. Depending on the position to be filled, a recruiter may want to include representatives from the support staff, such as instructional aides and secretarial/clerical staff. Many superintendents now include a governing board member on administrator interviewing committees. The superintendent usually participates as well.

The same concerns noted for a teacher interview committee carry over to the administrative committee. Because of the even greater diversity of the membership, an administrator candidate has a more difficult time attempting to address all views while not jettisoning his or her principles. You must accept as fact that not all members of your committee will value the very same qualities in the candidates.

As noted earlier, there are times when a parent has a problem at the classroom or building level and may need to have the problem addressed, not at the bottom of the hierarchy, but somewhere above that, perhaps at the superintendent level. For example, a parent may have a young child who had a bad experience with a specific classroom teacher and feels threatened about dealing with this teacher again if it concerns another one of his or her children.

In another case, a parent may have had a dispute with the principal and has reason to believe that the principal will now treat her or him unfairly. There are multiple reasons why solving a problem at a point other than at the bottom of the bureaucratic hierarchy makes sense. Yet, in the hundreds of administrative interviews I have conducted or monitored, not once has a candidate suggested that a solution to a problem be initiated anywhere other than at the bottom of the hierarchy! My sense is that this archaic philosophy has prohibited untold numbers of parents and students, nationwide, from receiving the services they deserve and have paid for. (This is especially true, I suspect, for those parents who are unable to articulate their needs or who do not know how to weave their way through the bureaucratic maze.)

Administrators, especially superintendents and building principals, need to understand that simply because a parent "goes away" does not mean she or he has been well served or that the parent has been served at all! Small wonder that a certain percentage of the parent constituency does not support our schools.

Therefore, a look at the makeup of the typical administrator interview committee makes it clear that there are diverse and potentially controversial views on the issue to where in the hierarchy a basic problem-solving effort should begin. Principals and teachers on an interviewing committee perceive this issue differently from how a superintendent or parent on the committee might look at it. Other issues that likely do not have consensus among the interviewers include policy on student discipline, comprehensive annual testing, homogeneous versus heterogeneous grouping, class-rank calculation, athletic team-cutting policy, selection process for valedictorian, dealing with a nonperforming or underperforming teacher, and many others.

It is into this cauldron of differences that the candidates must hurl themselves. Interviewers must remember that when they do not like an answer to a specific question, the administrator candidate actually is representing students, not staff or adults! On one hand, the candidate is expected to be a collaborative partner to the staff, but on the other he or she is also required to be its leader. Where do the interviewers want this candidate to be positioned on the administrator ability continuum? Do they want an administrator who hunkers down safely in the middle of the continuum, or do they want a principal who joins the ranks of courageous administrators who believe in doing what is right for students in the entire district? That decision remains solely with the interviewers!

Superintendent Interviewing Committees

During the past two or three years, a few governing boards have reverted to the old style of recruiting a superintendent: they exclude other parties from interviewing the candidates. Superintendent candidates find this the best of all worlds because their names are not made known publicly until the end of the process. There is no aspect of a job hunt that is more unsettling to a superintendent candidate, especially an experienced one, than that of having his or her name in the public arena early in the process. Any action that a hiring district is able to take to avoid early disclosure results in additional experienced candidates applying.

The perception in a candidate's home community is that if she or he came in second in a job hunt in another community, it is no better than coming in last. The candidate loses a little glitter back home. It is for this reason that in your role of recruiter you must make every effort to protect the names of superintendent candidates. The process described here, wherein a governing board excludes all other parties from the search, is the exception.

A superintendent search process remains one of the most complicated of all job-hunting procedures a governing board or its agent mounts. The interview process usually involves more than one committee. The general practice is for a governing board to act as one interviewing group and for a more diverse group to be engaged as a second interview committee. The diverse committee makeup varies from district to district, but it is a fact that most segments of the community are involved directly or through representatives. It differs somewhat from a committee established for a principal search in that the superintendent committee involves more individuals from civic, political, and community groups, including nonprofit agencies, that interact with the schools.

Although superintendent candidates usually are more comfortable with interviewing committees than teachers and administrators are, they all face the same dilemma in their need to exert caution in how they respond to loaded questions. As noted earlier, members on a diverse committee have different expectations. For example, the average citizen group comprises many subcultures. You have parents with children in school and parents with children yet to enter school; you have seniors who comprise adults without children, empty nesters whose kids are out of school, and older seniors with younger spouses with children still in school.

It is safe to say that each group has a different view on what the appropriate expenditure level should be for the school district. This is only one example of such diversity. The same can be said for every group represented on the committee. The areas of potential conflict are many.

ONCE AGAIN, "WHO IS ASKING THE QUESTION?"

Whether candidates are competing for a teacher position or for the position of superintendent of schools, the composition of the interviewing committee is vitally important to them. While the person asking the question is, at that moment, the most important person on the committee, each of the others has (or should have) a keen interest in the candidate's response. They are comparing responses to the standard they have established in their own minds (hopefully, with input from others). The representative from the local youth service agency has expectations for the schools that differ from those of the athletic department. The law enforcement agency may have decidedly different views on discipline than those of most principals. Representatives from town government have ideas for the use of tax dollars that differ from those of the school department. Each representative group poses different questions and expects different responses.

It is obvious that there will never be total consensus among the group regarding the "best" or "right" answers that a candidate provides to their questions. The diversity of thought around the table makes total consensus impossible. As the person responsible for facilitating the interview, you must not allow a single member's negative assessment to cause a viable candidate to be eliminated.

FINALLY, THE CORRECT ANSWER

What, then, are the appropriate answers that a candidate may offer? You certainly do not want a candidate who is overly tentative and plays to the audience. For a candidate to have no opinion is significantly worse than having strong but reasonable opinions. The solution to the dilemma posed is quite simple, but it requires personal courage. A candidate must rally the interviewers not around his or her responses but around him- or herself! The following personal example helps to undergird this point.

For twenty-five years, a resident of my community attended most of my budget meetings, at which time he would flail away at the school budget. During those years, he had also lodged a number of grievances with my athletic department. He had a rather contentious relationship with the school system. The year in which I retired, I took up golf at the same club at which he was a member. Knowing nothing about golf, I would stop at the course on the way home from work during my last year as superintendent and try hitting a few balls.

One day I was on the driving range armed only with a single, used seven iron. Next to me on the range was the person noted. He turned and asked me where my clubs were. I told him that I was a new member and had yet to buy clubs. At which point he said, "Here, use mine." I did so and thanked him. It is important to note that his clubs were new and expensive. It was a risk to hand them over to an absolute novice! Shortly thereafter he asked, "Where's your glove?" I told him I did not have one, at which point he handed me a spare he had in his bag. Then he offered a few suggestions on how to swing a golf club. Within a few weeks, he invited me to play golf with him.

The important lesson to be learned is that in all those years when he opposed my budget and had difficulty with the policies of my athletic department, he never opposed me personally! He knew what I stood for and respected it, even if he did not agree with my stance on an issue. The strength of my conviction was meaningful to him. I always treated him with respect, never expecting anything in return, and he in turn respected the commitment I had to students. To this day, thirty-five years later, he is still the consummate gentleman in his interaction with me and my wife. What I concluded from this experience is that a leader's constituents want him or her to have strength of character, a commitment to students, a moral and ethical quality. They want her or him to speak the truth. If a leader possesses these qualities, advocates will support her or him, adversaries will respect her or him.

Members of an interviewing committee, recognizing that the answers a candidate offers please some and perhaps annoy others because of the diversity of the committee, need to judge the candidates based on the depth of their beliefs that their only clients are the young children, the adolescents, and the young adults to be given to their care. Those in leadership roles—be they teachers in a classroom, building principals, or superintendents of schools—never please all constituents with their decisions. Conflict is inevitable. They can, however, stand for children, and for this stance they are likely to be rewarded and respected.

The lesson for all recruiters is that judgments about candidates must be based not on the fact that all interviewers must be accepting of their answers but that the answers given demonstrate one's commitment to education.

Chapter 14, "What You See Is What You Get," provides additional information to how to select the finalist.

⓭

WHAT YOU SEE IS WHAT YOU GET

When working with interviewers in preparation for their meeting with candidates, I conduct a thorough briefing session. In my role as consultant, I work mostly with governing boards, but as a superintendent I worked with my professional staff. Chapter 13 explains some of the details of a briefing session and what to look for in a candidate, but this chapter addresses one factor only—namely, the basic character of a candidate.

In thirty-five years of interviewing thousands of candidates and selecting hundreds for employment, I learned many valuable lessons. During those same years, I dismissed or encouraged many employees to leave, and from those experiences I learned still more.

I had the opportunity to work with approximately two hundred professional educators at any given time. It follows that I learned even more from them. The fact is that a wise superintendent accepts the fact that all subordinates are his or her mentors.

While this chapter focuses on the basic character of candidates, one overarching lesson recruiters must learn, especially if they are superintendents, is that they must learn from their past recruiting mistakes. Unless a recruiter is open to self-assessment and critique, the odds are that they learn nothing of value. It was from the early Greeks that subsequent leaders learned foolishly to kill the messenger. If superintendents and their recruiters kill the messengers, they also destroy the messages! Without the information contained within the messages, there is no effective way to improve the recruiting process. As difficult as it is to hear what has not gone well, your failure to listen will undermine your efforts. Do not destroy the messenger if you want to gain new knowledge about an important situation.

Leaving the messenger unharmed is easier said than done. Most leaders, especially superintendents, principals, and governing board chairs, acquire their positions of authority through strength of character. While most of them articulate the need for collaboration and sharing, many zealously guard their posts with the use of power. Suggestions are easily offered but often grudgingly accepted. I offer this opinion as an observation resulting from my personal experience and that of many fellow administrators. It is difficult for many leaders to accept criticism.

Without admitting failures, success becomes elusive. All this is by way of saying that anyone in a position to hire and fire must be willing to acknowledge recruiting errors.

So, if the overarching lesson is that one can use mistakes to learn, then what is the most important operational lesson learned and how do recruiters benefit from it? Simply put, what you as recruiter initially see in a candidate is most likely what you will get. There are exceptions, of course, but they are just that, exceptions. If a candidate appears to change character once hired, this most likely is due to your initial misreading.

I must emphasize to the interviewers that their primary task is to assess the basic personality of the candidate and not to be watchful for "correct answers." Answers can be easily altered; one's basic personality cannot.

A candidate who is invited to an interview after a thorough paper screening may know all of the answers! They may not be the answers sought, but they may be professionally satisfactory answers. Over time and with experience, they may have different answers, but that is true for all of us. What does not change over time is the basic personality of the candidate. It is for this reason that the primary mission of the interview committee is to engage the candidates in a way that allows them to project their basic personalities. Is this possible in one interview? It is

highly unlikely and is the reason why several interviews are often required. As a recruiter, you should never let time constraints interfere
with your assessment of a candidate.

The statement "What you see is what you get" was not meant to imply that after one sitting with a candidate you will learn all you need to
know. The first set of interviewers may not be sufficiently talented to
ferret out the information needed to make a decision about a candidate's
character and personality. It is possible that the time of day, the schedule, and the setting have their separate effects. There are days when
candidates may have serious personal or professional problems that are
weighing heavily on them so that their performance level is affected.
One interview may not be conclusive, but after three or more, people
reveal themselves for who they are.

Another anecdote is appropriate here. In a superintendent search
conducted a few years ago, seven candidates were invited to a search
committee comprising fourteen interviewers. The candidates were selected from a group of nineteen who had previously been screened, approximately half through preliminary interviews and through paper
screening. I was present at all of the interview sessions held between the
candidates and the search committee.

Following the first set of interviews with the search committee, three
candidates were selected for a second round of interviews with the same
fourteen interviewers. Although the process required that interviewers
not rank the candidates, there was a general belief, if unspoken, that one
candidate was leading the group.

There are two events that often occur at the first set of interviews between a search committee and the candidates. First, interviewers often
want to discover certain qualities in a candidate, even if such qualities
are not apparent or, if so, barely discernable. Second, approximately half
the time I am present at interviews, I do not agree with interviewers'
and governing boards' conclusions. This does not mean that they pre-
ferred unqualified candidates; instead, it often comes down to intuition
or chemistry. There is also the fact that, as a former superintendent,
rightly or wrongly, I think I am a better judge of a superintendent candidate than those who never served in the position.

In this search, I know the committee overestimated the qualities of
one candidate and underestimated the qualities of another. In the case

of the third candidate, I believe we all thought we saw the same qualities but needed another interview to make that decision.

What happened at the second set of interviews? A powerful turnaround took place. It provided a useful lesson that all recruiters can learn. Keep in mind a comment made earlier that it is dangerous to judge a candidate based on a single interview, no matter how certain you may be of your initial assessment. Following the first interviews, the members were requested to develop questions that focused on their areas of immediate concern. The second session was set up in an informal, conversational mode rather than structured in a formal interviewing format. The candidates were informed of this change beforehand and told they would have time to ask questions of the interviewers.

The candidates were informed that the interview would be one hour so that they could plan accordingly. (Candidates should always be informed of the time available to them.) In this case, they were informed that each of the interviewers would want to ask at least one question. Knowing this, the candidates can do the math: fourteen interviewers, sixty minutes for the interview, less ten minutes for candidates to ask questions, less time for opening and closing statements. This leaves the candidate with approximately forty-five minutes to respond to fourteen questions, or 3.2 minutes per question. The time a candidate consumes to respond to one question reduces the time available for other questions. I informed the three candidates of the concerns that came out of the first interview so that they could address them at the second interview if someone asked.

WHAT HAPPENED?

Candidate number 1. This was the candidate who was unofficially ranked number one after the first interview. The job was his to lose, which is what he did. This is what happened. The first question was a routine one that should have initiated a perfect interview. Instead, a rambling ten-minute monologue not only went nowhere but also exposed a poor vocabulary and an inarticulate educator. Answers were evasive, unclear, and seemingly unending. The interview, while it continued for the full hour, was essentially lost with his response to the first question. What was attributed to nervousness at the first interview was now viewed as an inability to stay on task, to answer questions succinctly, and to know when to stop. By all our later accounts, it was a painful interview.

Candidate number 2. This candidate ranked third after the first interview, and there was some debate whether he should be moved forward. The concern was that he seemed disheveled in his grooming, was too much the salesman, and had been too quick to leave his prior positions. At the second interview he addressed the points of concern, came across as a caring educator, and was, without doubt, of high intellect. His answers were succinct yet complete. He demonstrated an excellent command of English and left the committee with a sense of confidence that he could relate to any audience.

This was an impressive interview. Without the second interview, we would not have identified the sterling qualities he possessed. He did not receive this appointment, but when I called him to inform him of this decision, I also told him I would be pleased to represent him in another search and that he presented himself beautifully. I also shared with him that the reason he did not receive this appointment had nothing to do with his lack of qualifications; rather, it was because of candidate number 3's outstanding credentials.

Candidate number 3. This candidate was in second place at the end of the first round of interviews. Unlike candidate number 1, whom I knew from other work, and candidate number 2, whom I knew of but had never met, candidate number 3 was unknown to me before this search. Just as you, as a recruiter, must make an initial assessment, so did I. First, I paper-screened his application and found it to be in perfect order with all requested documents attached, including letters of reference and evidence of certification. The latter was a vital document since he was from out of state. Then I placed one phone call to a trusted colleague who was in a position to make a discreet inquiry about the candidate. Satisfied with the results of that reference check, I interviewed candidate number 3 for an hour in a one-on-one session.

As background, I had conducted focus sessions in the district and believed I knew exactly what the district required in its new superintendent. All of the recommended candidates possessed, in my opinion, the ability to run the district, but the essential question was, Which candidate could best meet the challenges that participants at the focus sessions described? It is one thing to manage a district, but it is quite another to propel it forward while addressing its expressed needs. Following my interview with the candidate, I thought he would be the choice if what I believed he had accomplished could be validated.

While he was somewhat nervous with the search committee at the first interview, he was more comfortable at the second interview. He put the committee at ease with his quiet, deliberate style. This was now the third time I observed him in an interview situation. He remained the same candidate throughout all three. This was a classic example of "What you see is what you get"!

Once the committee decided that this was the only candidate it would consider, I contacted five professionals who had worked with him not in his current district but in his prior district! In the many years I have conducted background checks, this was the most impressive case of a person being who he said he was, as evidenced by the five references I contacted. Comprehensive checks in his current district further validated this finding.

SIX LESSONS FOR RECRUITERS

1. First impressions are accurate only if they are validated after several contacts with a candidate.
2. Interviewers should not expect that a candidate's responses to questions will satisfy everyone, nor should they.
3. All candidates may pass the questions-and-answers quiz but may fail to meet other professional, moral, and ethical standards required.
4. Interviews are a valuable source of information as long as they are coupled with background checks.
5. The composition of an interview committee should be made known to the candidate.
6. Finally, what you see is what you get.

Chapter 15 provides guidelines that interviewers need to employ if they wish to be successful in their work.

ⓕ

GUIDELINES FOR INTERVIEWERS

In working with interviewing committees, it is necessary to prepare them for the group interviews. This requires conducting a comprehensive workshop before the first interview. The following guidelines are suggested for this task!

The tone of the interview begins the moment the chair of the committee greets the candidate and makes eye contact. When this occurs, the chair is in the unique position to create the appropriate climate for the interview. A friendly, professional, and warm welcome goes a long way to set a positive stage for the interview. The recruiter should carefully choose the person who chairs the interviewing committee, being confident that the chair can set the correct tone from the outset. Simply because one possesses an impressive title does not guarantee one an ability to chair an interviewing committee or provide an in-depth briefing.

Once the candidate enters the interviewing room, the chair should then introduce the candidate to the entire committee. Each member then introduces him- or herself. Each interviewer should have a name card that is large enough to be read by the candidate and identifies the person's present position.

If this is the first time the candidate is being interviewed, the chair must inform the candidate that the committee is taking no candidate questions at this time. In the event the candidate moves on to a second interview, he or she is then provided an opportunity to ask questions. There are three reasons for this condition being imposed. First, there is not sufficient time to answer questions during a first interview, when the interviewers are meeting many candidates and need to make a first-level cut. Second, once the candidate becomes the interviewer, the flow of the interview changes with the candidate taking charge! When this occurs, interviewers lose valuable time to raise their questions. Third, most of the questions the candidate asks are usually perfunctory, can be answered over the phone, and are usually questions not within the province of the members to answer.

The chair also informs the candidate that answers should be succinct since each member of the committee will ask at least one question and since the length of the interview is, for example, fifty minutes. The candidate can then do the math.

There is to be absolutely no food in the interview room, since candidates may be allergic to certain smells and foods. Coffee and cold drinks are permissible with water supplied to each candidate.

Members of the committee are prohibited from passing notes or whispering during an interview. Any reasonable person, especially a candidate, usually views both actions as negative and impolite.

If the interviewers are not provided with prepared questions, they should be expected to develop their own questions before the interviews. As part of the briefing, the chair must know which of the prepared questions are to be asked, the order in which they are to be asked, and who asks the first question of each candidate. The chair must also have the committee members review the questions that were prepared by individual members and that had not yet been seen by the full membership. The purpose of these guidelines is to be certain that the interview flows smoothly, that there is no embarrassment when silence follows an answer, and that all of the questions are appropriate and legal.

Interviewers ask only open-ended questions and refrain from asking questions that have answers available in the application materials. The exception is to ask clarifying questions about written materials that were submitted.

Committee members must refrain from asking convoluted questions that even their colleagues do not understand. They need to ask straightforward questions that do not merge two or more questions into one.

Interviewers must not provide the candidate with so much background to a question that they lead the candidate to the answer sought.

Questions that deal with personal concerns of an interviewer are not allowed. If an interviewer has an issue with the district, she or he should direct it to the appropriate administrator and not attempt to prompt the candidate to agree with her or his position.

It is important that the committee respect the fact that this time belongs to the candidate. It is not a forum for interviewers to express their personal views on issues raised with the candidate.

Whenever a candidate answers in the affirmative to a poorly stated question—such as "Have you ever terminated a teacher?"—it is appropriate to have the candidate follow up with specific dates, district, and circumstances.

Interviewers should not spend time asking a candidate how he or she handled a situation "back home"; rather, they want to know how he or she will address it in the present community given its unique set of conditions.

If the answer to a question is not understood by a committee member, the person needs to ask it again, in a different form, but not let it go unanswered.

Interviewers must not be impressed by where candidates have worked or where they attended college; rather, who they are and what they will bring to your district are what should impress. Districts interested in a pedigree may attract those with titles but not necessarily talent.

Interviewers must be aware of who falls within "protected groups," in terms of not discriminating against certain candidates by asking illegal questions. While federal statutes are clear, state statutes differ. Whoever is responsible for briefing the committee members needs to have legal counsel identify who falls within these protected groups in your state, and the chair must then make certain that members do not ask questions that infringe on the rights of a candidate on the basis of age, gender, ethnic/national origin, marital status, and so forth.

Every candidate has a right to privacy to the extent the law permits in the state where the interviewing takes place. Each candidate's name must not be made known publicly until the law requires it be made known. Interviewers must protect this right.

Under no circumstances are members of an interviewing committee to initiate their own background checks. The recruiter decides when that is to occur and who will conduct the checks.

The most important goal of the interviewers is to assess the candidate's basic personality. If the committee does not complete the goal of determining a candidate's basic character at either this interview or follow-up interviews, it will have failed in its mission.

Whoever asks a question has the responsibility to bring closure to the answer if the candidate appears to be rambling. An effective and proven method is to wait until the candidate takes a breath and at that moment to say, "Thank you." If this is done once or twice, the candidate will heed the message. It is not the chair's responsibility to limit the answers, although the chair may have to step in if an interviewer fails to do so.

The chair has the responsibility to guarantee each candidate equal time for the interview and equal treatment from committee members.

The chair is encouraged to set a tone wherein humor and levity are welcome.

Every courtesy must be extended to the candidate. Each must leave the interviewing room believing this to be the most thorough interview process ever personally experienced and that this community is one that honors education and candidates.

Each candidate who does not receive the appointment must believe that your district is a great district in which to work and the only reason she or he did not receive the appointment had nothing to do with the shortcomings of the interview process or the interviewers. Interviewers must be cognizant of the fact that the time they spend interviewing is an opportunity to win friends for the district from those who did not receive the appointment! Candidates always remember the courtesies extended to them and share their positive experiences with others. As a result of this reputation, others will apply for open positions.

In chapter 16, recruiters learn the unacceptable excuses that candidates offer in turning down an offer of employment.

16

ELIMINATING CANDIDATE EXCUSES

There comes a point in a search when the decision makers reach consensus that the ideal candidate has been identified and that the time has arrived to extend an offer of employment. The timing of the offer is critical and needs careful thought. More than one offer has been turned down when a candidate makes a last-minute decision because of the district's failure to clarify a number of factors that have historically derailed other job offers. Some of these factors are beyond the control of the employer, and therefore there is little to be done but to grin and bear the inevitable refusal of the candidate to accept a contract of employment.

There are a number of considerations that are definitely within the province of the hiring agent to settle before an offer of employment is extended. These considerations must be addressed long before the candidate reaches the final interview stage. You do not want to move a candidate forward if she or he is the least bit doubtful of accepting an offer. Indecision at this point can derail the entire search. Experience bears out the fact that most candidates who are waffling about an offer do not accept one if offered. If a candidate is prepared to withdraw from competition, she or he must do so early enough to allow another candidate to move up in the process. You also do not want interviewers spending time with a candidate who has already decided to withdraw and is merely going through the process for whatever reason, often an ego trip. There are candidates who apply for and hope to receive an offer but who have absolutely no intention of following through to the point of accepting employment. Many thrive on misleading recruiters. Others are just "exploring for the hell of it." A few thrive on the excitement of a search. Your task is to eliminate them as soon as possible.

Following are a few of the excuses candidates use to back out of a search at the end of the process. These are issues that need to be settled long before the district presents a contract of employment. If you fail to do so, you run the risk of heading for the finish line with no one with you! What are seen as excuses at the end of a search are legitimate and reasonable concerns if handled early in the process.

Salary. Often, a district allows itself to be painted into a corner when it concerns compensation. Job advertisements that state a range of compensation rather than a fixed amount can be misleading. A candidate has a right to know exactly what the compensation is. If benefits are part of a package, then these need to be itemized. To avoid this issue's becoming an excuse for the candidate to withdraw at the last minute, settle the matter at the outset and get a verbal agreement from the candidate that she or he understands and agrees to the compensation and benefit package. Governing boards, in spite of warnings from consultants, often leave the negotiating of the compensation package until after a vote has been taken to hire. Not only does the district leave itself vulnerable to a contract refusal, but it also gives up its negotiating strength since the candidate now takes control of the process! Settle the compensation early in the process. To do so accurately requires that the candidate examine her or his after-tax net and make a detailed comparison of current salary and benefits to those that you have offered.

As a recruiter who desires to have this candidate join your school system, you should assist her or him in making the comparison. It is obvious that the hiring district must settle all of the compensation details with the candidate as soon as possible. What the candidate overlooks, you should place into the discussion. There is nothing to be gained and a great deal to be lost if you hire a new employee who, upon arrival, feels misled.

Commute. It is interesting to observe how a candidate, at the last minute, "discovers" the length of a commute to the new district! This

discovery occurs at the last minute in spite of the fact that he or she
made the trip several times to appear for interviews. As a recruiter, settle this matter early in the process. Ask the candidate directly how long
it took to make the drive and then ask if the trip was made during approximately the same hours of a weekday that he or she would travel if
employed in your district. If the candidate has not, then strongly suggest
that he or she do so. Under no circumstance must you move a candidate
forward if he or she is uncooperative on this matter. Often, a candidate
uses his or her family as the reason why the commute will not work. The
fact of the matter is that this is a reasonable excuse but only if it is utilized at the beginning of the process. Using one's family to transfer responsibility is not a quality sought in a leader.

Health of parents. Most of the candidates applying for administrative
positions, especially superintendent positions, are usually in an age
range of forty to sixty years old. In many cases, their parents are getting
up there in age and increasingly look to their forty- to sixty-year-old children for assistance. As parents age, they tend to acquire illnesses or
handicaps. If there is a history of being a close-knit family, the children
are often concerned about leaving their parents. As a result, there is reluctance for administrative candidates to apply for positions that require
a physical move since the expressed needs of their families are important to them. At some time, most of us have faced or will face this same
dilemma.

It is inappropriate, if not illegal, for a recruiter to inquire about family matters as a condition of a search; therefore, it needs to be addressed
indirectly, unless the candidate introduces the subject. Just as was the
case of the "commuter," a candidate with aging parents or parents in
need knows at the outset of a search that a physical move could be an
impediment to accepting a job offer, and this should be discussed early
on in the process. When working with older candidates, I try to determine if this is a problem by listening carefully and paying attention to
any comment that the candidate makes relative to his or her parents. I
attempt to get at this issue with a general comment such as "Is there
anything of a personal or family nature that could interfere with your accepting a job offer with the district if one is extended to you?"

While the issue is one that can generate sympathy, the candidate has
a responsibility not to apply for a position if not intending to accept it if

later offered. Exceptions must always be made for the unexpected illness that may strike a family member. (Occasionally, a candidate from out of state may actually want to move to your district just to be with older parents who live in the area, thus increasing the probability of accepting the new job, if offered.)

Real estate values, equity in property, and moving expenses. I know of only a few candidates who have made a physical move into a less-expensive community! It just does not happen unless a candidate is in difficulty and needs to "disappear" from his or her current district or simply needs to be employed and will accept any position offered. Usually, a candidate who is promoting his or her career will make a move into a community where the compensation level is higher, whether it be into an upscale community or into a large city district. While the move is viewed professionally as a step up the career ladder, it also carries with it the possibility of an impending financial disaster. When a candidate is looking for a position, one of the first concerns, if not the first, is the salary level and benefit package, or the total compensation package.

This section begins with a discussion of how salary and benefits must be established early in the process. Whatever final figure is settled on, it is meaningless unless it complements the purchase price of real estate for a new home and the real cost of moving family and household to a new location. Even then, there is a tendency to total only the more obvious costs, such as a moving van, temporary housing, and transitional living expenses. From a purely economic point of view, that calculation does not represent the complete financial picture. A candidate needs to compute all expenses associated with the move, expenses that he or she would not have taken on if he or she had not made the move. He or she must take into consideration the culture into which the children will be placed and the financial demands that may be placed on the family as it attempts to integrate into the social fabric of the new community.

If a candidate moves a family into a high-cost community, he or she needs to have the financial resources that allow the family to enjoy what a spouse and children of a typical family in the community enjoy. If this is not done, you may hire and lose your candidate in a relatively short period. Children often feel victimized by a move, particularly when in their teen years, so a family may be forced to look for alternative ways to compensate for the move. These alternatives usually are costly. The lesson for recruiters and governing board members is that you have a responsibility to assist your candidate to make a sound financial decision to avoid future unpleasantness and dissatisfaction.

Spousal job dislocation. It is not unusual in the corporate world for a spouse of a CEO or high-ranking officer of a corporation to acquire a new position after a family has moved. While the position may not be in the same company, an influential corporate executive often has sufficient contacts and significant power to make this happen. This is not the case in local public education, although there are some exceptions, not all of them ethical (as noted earlier). For the most part, if one partner makes a physical move, the other follows but without any guarantee of a new position. The problem is especially acute when the other spouse earns as much or more than the partner who wants to make the move. There will, of course, be exceptions.

The issue for the recruiting district and its governing board is to make certain that the candidate has assessed the downside of a spouse not having a firm job offer when a move takes place. While the candidate must weigh what this means in financial terms, the recruiter needs to avoid having the candidate make a last-minute decision not to accept the position because of the lack of a job for the spouse. Whatever you do, you must not promise that you can find a job for a spouse when in fact you have no way to guarantee this happy event!

Pension benefits and concerns. Of all the excuses candidates use to turn down an offer of employment at the last minute, none is more frequently heard than that of inadequate pension benefits. Often, this is a legitimate reason since pension rights are important to an educator's retirement. For most educators, pension benefits from a state-funded retirement system are a major source of income upon retirement. As is the case with other excuses, it is a matter of timing. A recruiter and a governing board are not only remiss but negligent if they fail to explore this matter with an out-of-state candidate early in the process. This is the most challenging of all issues facing most out-of-state candidates.

There is no single, national pension system for public school employees. The primary retirement system is provided through the state pension systems, with each state operating under a different set of highly complex eligibility rules and providing vastly different payouts upon retirement. While there may occasionally be a somewhat smooth transition from one state to another, for the most part the process is confusing and expensive. Most candidates never commit the time to explore this matter until they are well into a search. The recruiter or governing board must take an active role is exploring this with any candidate who appears qualified to be appointed to the position.

A recent experience with a governing board serves as a warning to all board members engaged in recruiting a superintendent, as it pertains to pension benefits. I was working on a search where a large number of out-of-state educators were contacted to determine if they had an interest in a particular superintendent position. Almost all of the out-of-state contacts were the result of cold calls; consequently, the initial interest of most candidates was superficial, but they had nothing to lose if they agreed to have a conversation about the opening.

As I examined the list, there was little doubt in my mind, based on many years of experience, that none of the out-of-state candidates who expressed an interest in this position would have taken time to explore the pension system in this particular state. When talking to them, most claimed a general idea, but all would have failed the most elementary of tests as to how the pension system really worked.

As it turned out, none of the candidates from out of state had any idea of the complexities of the state pension system, with the exception of a few from out of state who had originally worked in the state where the search was conducted. However, even then, they had completed no detailed homework and had little or no idea of the pension consequences of moving across state lines.

Within this large group who had been contacted, there were many outstanding candidates, some who were professionally prepared to move and others who did not intend to move because they possessed outstanding compensation packages in their current positions.

The message for all governing boards is this: Do not waste your time and that of your recruiting staff pursuing out-of-state candidates unless the candidates can afford to incur whatever losses may accrue to them because of the pension issue. Then make absolutely certain that, as a governing board, you are in a position to compensate the candidates for any such loss. Since neither the governing board nor those they employ are experts in the pension benefit field, there may be a need to hire a pension expert to help ease the way. But it must be done early in the process, at that moment you believe a qualified candidate has been identified.

Another warning for governing boards is this: If a candidate accepts your offer and is willing to relocate to your state and incur permanent pension losses, you need to conduct a serious due diligence on the person's background, for what candidate would take such a loss if they did not have to? The most likely candidates for the position are those who need to leave where they are or those who do not intend to remain for any length of time.

In chapter 17, recruiters are taught how to provide a candidate with a well-defined starting line and a clearly visible finish line.

①

THE STARTING AND
FINISHING LINES

The typical interview, whether it takes place in a one-on-one session or in a group setting must be carefully structured so that the candidate receives approximately 95 percent of the interviewing response time with the interviewers limited to 5 percent, which is sufficient for them to ask their questions. It is vital that the questions asked provide the interviewers the opportunity to learn something of significance about the candidate; otherwise, the time spent together serves no worthwhile purpose.

LITMUS TEST QUESTIONS

At this stage of the process, a candidate knows or should know the answers to all questions that deal with important educational issues. If not, then the recruiter may have brought forth the wrong candidate. It is true that a candidate may not know all of the specific details about your district, but in the final analysis how important is that information? Usually, it is statistical data that are always available when needed. It is expected that a qualified candidate has done considerable personal research about the district, but that does not guarantee that he or she will have mastered all of the minor details. A candidate's mastering of details about a district is hardly the measure of the man or woman as it relates to his or her ability to lead the district or school.

All too often an individual interviewer wants to judge the fate of a candidate based on a response to a single question. This tends to occur when a district administers a litmus test–type question based on a single overriding issue, such as a candidate's position on gifted education. A governing board may be of the mind that the candidate must share the same philosophy it does or otherwise be effectively removed from the search. I cannot recall any one question having been asked during my thirty-five years as a superintendent and consultant that justified a candidate's elimination!

I know of governing boards that during a search allowed each of its members to ask their favorite questions, the answers to which moved the candidate along, stalled the candidate in the search, or removed the candidate from contention. In other words, the candidate is expected to provide a "right" answer. These questions and answers are essentially litmus tests.

Depending on your point of view, it may not speak well of any board that has such a hard and fast opinion about a specific program or activity that it is willing to eliminate a candidate based on the "wrong answer" to one or more philosophical, rhetorical, or controversial questions. A governing board with such a mind-set may also run the risk of advertising to all candidates for all positions in its district that "It's our way or the highway." If a governing board wants a puppet as its leader, it should advertise for one.

Examples of Litmus Tests

Board member number 1: "Alice, as you may know, we have a fledgling program for the gifted in our schools. We are now at the stage in its development where we believe a decision needs to be made as to how it should be organized. Please share with us how you would organize the program for the gifted if you are appointed superintendent."

A possible litmus test answer: "I believe that the gifted can only be served if they are enrolled in a dedicated program. A pullout program, where students spend some portion of their day with average students, is limited in value and generally a waste of time for those students who are this talented."

Board member number 2: "Arthur, in reading your application materials, I found only limited information as it relates to your effectiveness in the supervision and evaluation of personnel. As you can appreciate, the evaluation of personnel in this district can be overwhelming considering the number of administrators we employ and the fact that a few administrators are not pulling their weight. Can you share with us what your experience has been in terminating administrators or moving them out of a district?"

A possible litmus test answer: "I have had great experience and success in firing or getting rid of administrators."

Board member number 3: "Jessica, given your prior experience as a curriculum specialist and your understanding of the traditional process employed to develop outstanding curriculum material, what do you see as the respective roles of the curriculum specialist, building principals, superintendent, and the governing board?"

A possible litmus test answer: "I believe that principals should have limited input, that in-house curriculum specialists should be responsible for the professional development that is required of staff to implement a new curriculum, that the governing board should be the major player, and that the superintendent should implement the board's decisions."

These are but three possible areas that may be "tested," but obviously, any function or program may be the target of such testing. Governing boards and recruiters who use such litmus tests to judge candidates most likely conclude such a search only if they can employ educational leaders who are in lockstep with a governing board. It will employ a follower while the staff had anticipated a leader.

Whether a governing board recruiting for a superintendent or a recruiter seeking teachers and other administrators, all should make the process easy on themselves by announcing the district's litmus test positions as part of the vacancy announcements and interview only those who are in accord with the district's positions. A governing board, being duly elected, has voter and statutory authority until the next election to establish a litmus test philosophy, even if it runs counter to the governance model used by most governing boards.

EFFECTIVE STRATEGIES TO
IDENTIFY THE REAL CANDIDATE

The most revealing interviews are those structured in such a way that interviewers, especially superintendents and governing board members, come to identify the real person behind the answers. A format that uses only questions and answers fails to identify the important qualities a candidate possesses. It can never discover what a candidate actually stands for. What you learn with the traditional questioning format is only what is provided in the answers and little more. There are two proven strategies that help enormously in learning much more about a candidate.

The Opening Statement

Of these two strategies, the opening statement is the most difficult for a candidate to handle, not because he is unable to articulate who he is and what he stands for, but because the candidate runs the risk of not knowing when to stop talking. Earlier, I mentioned the situation wherein a candidate rated number one after the first interview ended in last position because of his response to the first question posed at the second interview, a response that was similar to an opening statement. However, properly used, an opening statement is a powerful tool for a governing board to use and is a valuable opportunity for the candidate. Every recruiter, regardless of the administrative position to be filled, would be well advised to implement this strategy.

This is how an opening statement should work. The chair of the interview committee informs the candidate beforehand, usually while greeting him or her before the interview, that she or he will be provided two to three minutes at the beginning of the interview to make an opening statement and two to three minutes at the end of the interview for a closing statement. Most interviewers, especially governing board members, do not utilize an opening statement because they are often unaware of its value. For those who want to utilize this strategy, the most effective way for the chair to introduce the opening statement is with a brief comment: "Sarah, we have set aside two to three minutes at the outset of this interview for you to share with us any thoughts about yourself that will give the committee an insight into who you are and the things that are important to you. I ask that you be succinct, however."

I prefer this simple opening because it provides the candidate an opportunity to set the tone for the interview and because the chair has established the parameters. At this moment, she is more than just "the first of five candidates being interviewed." She is onstage before an inquisitive audience. What a wonderful opportunity to define her character and values. Moreover, for the committee, it engages the candidate in an informal and personal way. This candidate could be your next superintendent, principal, or teacher of your children! Do you not want to know who she is?

After the question-and-answer session is concluded, there needs to be some opportunity for closure. So often, the ending has an anticlimatic feel to it. It is as though some element is missing. In fact, an important element is missing! It is a closing statement. Just before closure, the chair needs to provide the candidate an opportunity to complete the interview.

The Closing Statement

Every recruiter, whether an employee recruiter or the governing board, should require that all interviews at every level of the organization conclude with a closing statement. Unlike the opening statement that is framed somewhat by the chair's lead-in statement, the closing statement is left totally to the discretion of the candidate. All the chair needs to say is "Sarah, we want to afford you two or three minutes at this time to leave us with any final thoughts, filling in where our questions didn't tread and sharing any personal information that you believe makes you the perfect candidate for our district."

When working with candidates rather than with a district or governing board, I urge candidates to give serious thought to both the opening and the closing statement in the event that they are provided an opportunity to make either before an interviewing committee. It may be that they are never asked for either, an unfortunate shortcoming of the interview, but the process of thinking about those two comments is nevertheless helpful to candidates as they respond to routine questions. Too often candidates fail to reveal themselves, losing an opportunity to tell interviewers who they really are while trying to dodge the bullets that come in the form of questions from a diverse group. As noted so often in this guide, there is no way to satisfy all interviewers; therefore, candidates need to explain themselves. The questions and answers will long be forgotten, but the professional and personal impression a candidate leaves with interviewers will not. The exceptions, of course, are the governing board members or superintendents who use questions as a litmus test to assure themselves that a candidate agrees with their philosophy of education or style of management.

Given that these district leaders possess such parochial views, they may not be the districts or superintendents for whom a candidate should work. Whatever the title of the recruiter, the more open you are to a candidate's views, irrespective if they agree with yours, the more you will learn about the candidate. This places you in a better position to decide if a candidate is the right person for the open position.

Governing boards and superintendents need to remind themselves constantly of the purpose of an interview. Is it to determine if a candidate has the correct answers? If so, this is folly since there are no correct answers to most questions in education. If there were "correct" answers, then why are we constantly changing our philosophy about how English or mathematics should be taught? Did we not have the correct answer when we adopted the last revision for our math series? Are we not still debating whether full inclusion is an appropriate strategy? What is the correct answer to that question? If the person asking the question would keep in mind that a question is only the starting point of an educational journey, then the candidate's answer will be appreciated as being but one possible route to reach the destination. If this agreement is reached, then both parties can use the time together to decide if they will make an effective team.

Chapter 18, "Dollars and Cents," outlines for governing boards the process to determine the compensation to be paid to new employee.

⓲

DOLLARS AND CENTS

This chapter is designed primarily for governing board members who, after a minimum of two interviews and a preliminary background check, have narrowed the search for a superintendent to one or two choices. Long before a board votes to elect a new superintendent, it is vital that all of the financial details are settled. Most governing boards fail to heed this advice and, consequently, lose their negotiation advantage with the person ultimately selected.

As background, a governing board must appreciate that the marketplace plays a significant role in determining a compensation package. In a tight labor market, the seller has the upper hand. In a market with large numbers of qualified candidates available, the buyer has the advantage. In this current decade, it is a seller's market. Outstanding superintendents are in a position to determine the contents of a compensation package. If a board has cause to reach down to the next level where there are competent but not outstanding candidates, a board has an improved opportunity to negotiate effectively.

Having negotiated on behalf of a number of governing boards, I have learned that there is a need to establish a baseline from which to initiate discussions with the favored candidates. It is best to begin by assuming that if a candidate currently enjoys an outstanding compensation package, it becomes the baseline from which negotiations are initiated. Some negotiators like to spar with a candidate on this issue, but I have found this strategy to be a waste of time. No outstanding candidate is about to lose benefits currently enjoyed. There is little to be gained and much to lose if negotiators attempt to reduce or eliminate benefits that a candidate already possesses. It is not an effective way to begin negotiations. If not careful, you will lose the candidate.

Another bit of background information is valuable for a governing board. I mentioned that it is vital that a board settle the compensation package long before a vote to select a superintendent is taken. Based on extensive experience, most boards fail to do this either because the chair is negligent in appointing a committee to work with the consultant to accomplish this task or a committee appointed to perform this task fails to complete its work. This is negligence of the highest order in negotiating a contract. If a vote is taken without a mutually agreed-on contract, the governing board loses its negotiating strength and the candidate gains control over the process. If you have an outstanding candidate, she or he may simply walk away from the negotiating table leaving the board with little more than embarrassment and a vacant position.

If there are two or more finalists and the board wishes to conduct two or more site visits and the candidates agree, then the board must secure financial data from each of the candidates and then develop and secure an agreement from each on a draft contract of employment before the board agrees to a site visit! In other words, the governing board wants each of the finalists to settle on a draft contract, complete with the compensation package, before a commitment is made to visit their districts or take a vote to select. I suggest the use of a financial data request form. The following is a form that my firm developed and that has been used successfully.

FINANCIAL DATA REQUEST FORM

Name:_____

Home Phone:_____

Business Phone:_____

Cell Phone:_____

E-mail:_____

Please complete this form and fax it to: (fill in the name and address of the person to receive the completed form)

If you are currently employed as a superintendent of schools, you must attach a copy of your current employment contract. If you are not currently employed, attach a copy of your last contract.

Basic salary for 2004–2005 (do not include other compensation, such as annuities or paid insurance premiums):

$_____

Basic salary for 2005–2006, if known at this time (do not include any other compensation, such as annuities or paid insurance premiums):

$_____

Annuities for 2004–2005 that are employer paid:

$_____

Annuities for 2005–2006 that are employer paid, if known at this time:

$_____

Premiums for 2004–2005 for whole life policies that are employer paid:

$_____

Premiums for 2005–2006 for whole life policies that are employer paid, if known at this time:

$_____

Face value of any term insurance for 2004–2005 that is employer paid:

$_____

Face value of any term insurance for 2005–2006 that is employer paid, if known at this time:

$_____

Does your employer pay any portion of your contribution to the state pension system? If so, what is the amount for 2004–2005?_____

What is the amount for 2005–2006, if known at this time?_____

Monthly car allowance for 2004–2005 (do not include amount paid to you on a voucher on the basis of actual miles traveled): $_____

Monthly car allowance for 2005–2006, if known at this time (do not include amount paid by voucher based on actual miles traveled):
$_____

Vacation days allowed per year: _____
Can vacation days accumulate?_____ If yes, how many?_____
Are you paid for unused vacation days upon leaving the district?
_____
How many days are you paid for?_____
What amount are you paid for each unused vacation day on leaving the district?_____
Are unused vacation days reimbursed at the end of each year?_____
How many are allowed?_____
What amount are you paid per vacation day: $_____

Sick days allowed per year:_____
Can sick days accumulate?_____ If yes, how many?_____
Are you paid for unused sick days on leaving the district?_____
For how many of these days are you paid?_____
What amount are you paid for each sick day on leaving the district?
_____

Dollar amount you are required to contribute monthly to your employer for health benefits. (Do not include life insurance.)

Please list by type of insurance:

2004–2005   2005–2006
Health: $_____   Health: $_____
Dental: $_____   Dental: $_____
Disability: $_____   Disability: $_____
Other: $_____   Other: $_____
Please explain: Please explain:

If you are not accepting health, dental, disability, or other insurance coverage, are you given a monthly or annual stipend in lieu of such coverage: _____

What is the monthly amount?_____ or annual amount?_____

In addition to submitting your current or last contract of employment, please submit copies of all federal 1099 forms for the year of your latest tax return.

Please list on a separate sheet any other benefits you currently enjoy, and attach a dollar amount to them.

The data on this form, confirmed by a copy of the candidate's current contract of employment, affords the governing board an improved opportunity to develop a new contract of employment for the candidate.

Chapter 19, "Validation 101," assists the recruiter to validate all information pertaining to the candidate.

19

VALIDATION 101

In the course of a search for candidates for positions in education, the district receives considerable information either directly from the candidate or from secondary sources. There is a need to validate all data received. The following is an examination of the types of data received and how a recruiter must look at them. While the categories vary somewhat on a teacher application, the general approach to examining data remains the same. Validation 101 may appear to be overkill, but there have been a sufficient, if rare, number of cases where high-profile personalities have presented fraudulent data. It is best to spend the time being proactive rather than being reactive once the media discover a serious flaw in the finalist's credentials! This is not an uncommon occurrence.

Compensation and contract information. Chapter 18 describes the financial data request form used to collect compensation information. It also noted that the recruiter should request a copy of the candidate's current contract as a way to validate what is provided on the application.

Professional experience. Every recruiter must require that dates of employment be listed using both month and year so that every month is accounted for, starting with the date the undergraduate degree was earned. Next, you need to have a contact name for every employer listed if you intend to validate that the experience listed is accurate and that it took place when and where noted.

Educational background. Most applications permit candidates to submit copies of transcripts with the requirement that official transcripts with the registrar's seal are submitted before the first interview takes place. As a safeguard, a recruiter may also want to request a copy of all diplomas as a check on the transcripts. As part of the educational background check, a district needs to take careful note of where degrees were earned and then determine whether the institution is accredited or, if not, whether it is a "diploma by mail" operation. The last thing a recruiter needs is to have the media or another disgruntled candidate discover that your finalist did not earn a claimed degree from an accredited institution.

Letters of reference. While rare, there are cases where a candidate writes her or his own references and submits them as though written by others. To check the veracity of the letters, a recruiter should contact the authors of all letters of reference, in particular those that you view as the most important and written by those whose opinions played some role in a contract being offered.

Names of references. Most applications require, in addition to letters of reference, other names that may be used as references. The only names that are important are those of persons who can speak to the professional background of the candidate. If such names are missing, the recruiter should ask that the candidate submit new and appropriate names.

Certifications. It is essential to determine if a candidate holds or is eligible to hold certification appropriate to the position in the state of application. Most candidates want to believe that if they hold certification in one state, other states will automatically certify them for a similar position in the new state. This, of course, is not the case in most states. If you as recruiter have an interest in a candidate, in spite of the fact that he or she did not take the time to determine eligibility, then you have to contact your state certification office to do so.

Signature and date. All applications must be signed as a way to commit the candidate to the information submitted and as a way for the employer to terminate a contract if it is later determined that the information submitted was false.

Chapter 20, "Don't Call Us, We'll Call You," outlines the recruiter's responsibility to keep candidates informed of their status.

(20)

DON'T CALL US, WE'LL CALL YOU

I have conducted educational searches for thirty-five years either as a school superintendent or search consultant. Both institutions, combined, processed tens of thousands of applications. To the best of my knowledge, all candidates who submitted an application received a reply noting their status in the search. If someone did not receive a reply, it was an oversight or human error, not because of an unwillingness to respond. Every organization that solicits applications has an obligation to reply to all candidates. If a candidate, whether qualified or not, takes the time to apply for a position, then the institution has a responsibility to reply. The reply, in the majority of cases, is not always the reply sought, but it fulfills a need that a candidate has to be kept informed.

A word of caution is appropriate for the recruiter on this matter. While every applicant should receive a reply, you need not respond to those who submitted only a partial application, usually a cover letter or a resume. To do so would overburden all human relations departments regardless of their size.

Most school systems in the country are classified as small but still receive thousands of applications every year. There is every reason to believe that, considering the number of applications relative to the size of the human relations department, small districts process proportionately the same number of applications as large urban districts. The point to be made is that the burden on a small district to respond may be the same as the burden on a large district; therefore, neither has an excuse to ignore candidates.

In my practice, I utilize at least six different letters to inform candidates of their status. Today, with the sophisticated technology that is available, a district is able to utilize dozens of different form letters, depending on what reply is appropriate. The following are some of the form letters we utilize:

Acknowledge receipt of an application
Rejection sent to internal candidates
Rejection sent to external candidates
Rejection sent to those interviewed but not offered a position
Rejection sent to those who did not possess proper certification
Acceptance sent to those offered a contract

These letters are but a sample; there are many variations, depending on the needs of the district. The important point is that you must reply in a timely fashion! The most important letter you send is that which informs a candidate who has been interviewed that he or she is not being moved forward in the process. It is not that the other letters are unimportant; it is just that a candidate who has been interviewed has a greater emotional investment in the job hunt than those not interviewed. The letter needs to be straightforward and written with care so as not to diminish a candidate's candidacy.

If your district has a philosophy that sends a message of "Don't call us, we'll call you," it will eventually be a loser in the recruiting business. This is an attitude that communicates to prospective candidates that each is but another number, logged in and soon forgotten. Word spreads quickly among educators that certain districts operate unprofessionally. When this happens, a district loses traction in attracting future candidates. In an era where there is a shortage of qualified candidates for literally all positions in education, a district needs to assume a stance that encourages prospective candidates to apply. A district's attitude should be "We'll try to call you even before you call us!"

There is another practical reason to handle candidates professionally. For most positions, there are several candidates, but there is only one who is the most qualified. There also is the situation where you have several qualified candidates but only one of whom can be employed since there is only one opening. Were the situation such that two positions were available, you would hire one of those rejected. However, because there is only one opening, a qualified candidate will be "temporarily lost" to the district. You need to build into your recruiting guidelines a method wherein those who are temporarily lost can be quickly contacted when another appropriate opening occurs. It may be that the candidate accepted employment elsewhere, but your effort will result in positive public relations. Over the years, I used this system of callbacks effectively in hiring candidates who were passed over a year or two earlier. For a callback approach to be effective, you must not lose track of qualified candidates who were not offered employment the first time around.

Every recruiter knows that when there are two or more outstanding finalists, the decision to hire one over another is often a matter of the successful candidate's having either a small edge or "chemistry." In another month or year, when a new position opens or is created, the edge or chemistry may have changed, and the best man now becomes the groom and the bridesmaid now becomes the bride!

Earlier, I make the point that a superintendent who does not remain in a position for a reasonable period often does not think long term about a new recruiting system. When that occurs, it remains for the designated recruiter, whether it is a central office administrator or the governing board, to step in and create just such a long-term recruiting program. Callbacks are one aspect of an effective recruiting program.

Chapter 21, "How Did Underperformers Come to Be Hired?" explains the necessity for a recruiter to examine how underperformers come to be hired in a school district.

(21)

HOW DID UNDERPERFORMERS COME TO BE HIRED?

The introduction emphasizes the need for a school district to implement a recruiting program that respects all candidates regardless of race, color, gender, religion, or other persuasions. The chapter also stresses that an effective recruiting program needs to emphasize strength, the strength of superintendents and governing boards to withstand the pressures of patronage, favoritism, and other unethical influences, from without and within the system. I experienced such a program in my first teaching assignment, in a lighthouse school district, which proved to be a memorable and valuable professional experience.

Today we refer to districts with the same goals as those lighthouse districts as high-performing organizations. They have strong test scores, a high percentage of students taking advanced placement courses, an extensive and inclusive curriculum, and graduates who attend the most competitive and prestigious colleges and universities. These districts usually have the most competitive salary schedules in their region, and they employ the most competent staff, those who have outstanding educational backgrounds with advanced degrees in core subjects. Outstanding districts, regardless of the nomenclature used to describe them—past and present—have well-developed recruiting programs that engage in effective hiring. The leaders of these districts understand that unless you have a powerful staff, nothing much of value occurs in the schools.

Nevertheless, as well intended as a district may be in its effort to establish a noteworthy recruiting system, there are occasions where the system fails and unqualified candidates are employed. When this occurs, several questions come to mind. Where were the safeguards? Who failed to act appropriately? What aspects of the recruiting system did not measure up to the district's expectations? When did the process break down? What was the nature of the pressure or favoritism that led to a poor decision?

There are several points in a recruiting process where errors of judgment can occur: when reference checks are inadequate, where pressures to appoint favorites are applied, and when those responsible for recruiting do not make sound judgments. Then again, not everyone employed in public education has an ethical standard compatible with the recruiting policy of the board or administrative practices of the superintendent!

Consequently, what practices does a district employ to ensure that future recruiting efforts are successful? What strategies can be employed that encourage reflection to view the future? What mechanism is available to audit the past performance of the recruiters? I suggest a simple and direct system of accountability that identifies all teachers currently employed in a district who should not have been employed in the first place or, if employed, should not have been retained!

The suggested system requires a degree of self-assessment on the part of all who participated in the hiring process because they must step forward and acknowledge that a poor hiring or retention decision was made. It also requires a superintendent who does not hold trials. If a leader of a high-performing district expects subordinate administrators to be truthful and forthcoming about their marginally competent hires, then the leader must be willing to listen constructively to the truth and not cast blame. It is from the forthrightness of administrators that one learns valuable lessons.

The current evaluation practice in education is to give considerable attention to those who have not yet acquired tenure, usually teachers with less than four years of experience. This cohort includes beginning teachers without experience and experienced teachers new to the district.

An examination of most school district evaluation plans bears out that the highest percentage of time spent on evaluation efforts is dedicated to the new hires and the nontenured staff. Tenured staff members usually escape the rigorous aspects of the evaluation system that is employed for new hires. This condition exists because teacher organizations have a powerful voice in how evaluation systems are constructed. The most senior teachers usually possess the leadership positions in the teacher organizations. Aspects of an evaluation plan that focus on the more senior staff are usually directed at those who are the "least competent" and "incompetent." Those above the "least competent" level— that is, barely treading water professionally—are generally safe from serious scrutiny!

There are two reasons for this. First, the pressure that the public imposes on school budget administrators makes it difficult for a superintendent to hire qualified supervisory personnel. The public generally views such personnel as unnecessary overhead. Second, building-level administrators are inclined to "put up with them," with "them" being those educators barely above the least competent level, because most remediation efforts have proven futile. The irony is that it is the failure to scrutinize why the least competent employees were hired in the first place that presents a current danger to a district's recruiting plan! Unless and until a district reviews its past practices, it may commit itself to repeating past errors.

Educators and public alike argue that districts must have a comprehensive evaluation plan for nontenured teachers and generally support these efforts. Nevertheless, it is equally important to review the hiring practices that were utilized in the hiring of nontenured teachers who later are recommended for nonrenewal. It is also critical that a district review the hiring practices that led to the hiring of underperforming tenured teachers.

I suggest an effective method for identifying all underperforming staff members as a way to improve the district's recruiting program. The superintendent, whether of a district or an area within a large urban center, needs to develop a formal system to identify underperformers, the purpose being to determine how and why they were employed in the first place! While one would assume that every district analyzes the performance of all staff members every year with the objective of improving recruiting efforts, my thirty-five years of experience dictates otherwise. What does occur is the creation of substantial written material that describes what evaluators have witnessed, but the documentation does not examine why and how an employee, now an underperformer, was hired! This chapter addresses the examination phase, the "why."

Every third year, at a minimum, all administrators in the district should be required to identify any staff member who, if the clock could be turned back, would not have been hired, would not have been granted tenure, and would not have been retained. This examination must be independent of the formal evaluation plan! As noted, the typical evaluation plan describes to the reader what is occurring with the employee at that moment in time, but it does not explain why the underperforming employee got here or is allowed to remain here. The evaluation phase answers the "what" while the examination phase focuses on the "why." No staff member should be exempt from the examination phase.

The size of the district determines the extent to which administrators are able to identify such employees for examination, but at a minimum, they should scrutinize their own staff. They also should be encouraged to identify teachers even if they are not members of administrators' own staff. Administrators who have been in a district for any length of time often have a network through which they receive information that would lead them to believe that a staff member in another school should not have been hired. This is especially true of central office administrators who have contacts in many buildings.

While there is a risk that some of what administrators learned through their personal networks may be based on scuttlebutt, other administrators should be able to clarify any hearsay information. Prior experience with this process indicates that successful administrators with extensive experience in a district have a good sense of who the marginal teachers are in other buildings.

Each administrator needs to view this exercise as a valuable tool for the district, one that allows the superintendent to identify what needs to be reconfigured in the hiring process to ensure that only highly qualified classroom teachers are employed. As noted earlier, even the best recruiting plan has fissures that allow an unacceptable number of marginal candidates to be hired.

The examination process begins with each administrator receiving a complete list of all staff members in his or her school, district, or unit within a large district, as determined by the superintendent. The list includes all classroom teachers and all nonclassroom staff, such as counselors, therapists, and social workers. No one is exempt. The administrators then identify all underperformers as described earlier, regardless of years of experience. When an administrator suggests a name, he or she must be prepared to speak to the conditions that allowed the staff member to be employed and/or retained in the district.

The superintendent would then hold a meeting with her or his administrators to discuss the personnel so identified. For large districts, administrators would need to be sensibly assembled in keeping with the organizational structure. The smaller the group, the more effective the meeting. There is no one effective way to group administrators; therefore, the superintendent must organize the meeting in a way deemed most effective. Once the meeting convenes, the administrators share with each other the conditions that led to the employment of underperformers, which so happens to be the subject of chapter 22, "The Vetting Process: Anecdotes and Lessons Learned."

THE VETTING PROCESS: ANECDOTES AND LESSONS LEARNED

In chapter 21, I focus on conditions within the recruiting process that allow candidates to be hired who later prove to be underperformers. I further note that the typical evaluation system for employees is based on portraying what is currently occurring between a marginal or underperforming teacher and his or her students and that the system does not consider the conditions that led to the employment of the employee. This chapter addresses the latter point.

When a superintendent convenes a meeting with administrators to identify underperforming staff members, as suggested in chapter 21, it follows that administrators will share anecdotes about their staff members, anecdotes that are valuable to a district's efforts to reshape its recruiting program. The value that is derived from the session is in direct relationship to the forthrightness and integrity of the administrators. In turn, their forthrightness is a function of the openness of the superintendent to hear "bad" news and not engage in retributions. Underperformers in a district must be identified, for these are teachers who literally cheat children out of a quality education.

All of the teachers and the conditions under which they are hired reflect what superintendents typically experience across the nation. At some point, a recruiting system fails students. The anecdotes of teachers described in this chapter are valuable lessons for recruiters. The anecdotes will be familiar to most recruiters.

ANECDOTE I

High school mathematics teacher number 1. His principal, unhappy with the teacher's behavior and its impact on students, suspects that the teacher exhibited a similar attitude when he was employed in his previous district. He also believes that if a thorough and professional background check had been conducted, it would have uncovered the teacher's true behavior. The teacher's hiring now raises several questions. Was the new district purposely misled? Did the teacher's previous principal and chairperson deceive the recruiter? Why did the recruiter not question more thoroughly the reason the teacher left his prior district after only three years? Was the teacher nonrenewed or encouraged to leave because of his poor attitude? Was a site visit conducted? Was the telephone reference check inadequate?

Lesson I

Poorly structured and conducted background checks and the absence of a site visit inevitably result in marginal teachers being employed. There is little in a person's background that cannot be uncovered if those who conduct reference checks and site visits are appropriately trained. Too often, a human relations department leaves background checks and site visits to those who are not qualified to conduct them.

ANECDOTE 2

High school mathematics teacher number 2. An examination of her undergraduate transcript provides clear evidence of a poor academic record. Complaints registered about her are not personal in nature; rather, they are directed at classroom performance. Because of her marginal performance, she is assigned exclusively to general mathematics classes. She has a record of having difficulty with classroom management. She was hired at a time when there was a shortage of mathematics teachers, and she was not considered outstanding at the time of hiring. Since her employment, she has performed at an average or below-average level.

Lesson 2

Quality undergraduate work must be a baseline requirement for employment, with no exceptions! All too often a transcript indicates an average academic record, but a detailed examination often reveals a below-average rank in core subjects, the very disciplines to which a teacher is assigned. This is a special concern with middle school and high school teachers who must teach in a specific discipline. A district must not let a teacher shortage force it into hiring average candidates. It is better to rely on long-term substitutes.

ANECDOTE 3

High school chemistry teacher. She is an excellent classroom teacher but a divisive member of the faculty, one whose tantrums and disagreeable outbursts outweigh admirable classroom accomplishments. The administration is constantly intervening in faculty disputes initiated by her. She is usually the first to complain and the last to volunteer. Those who have known her since she began employment in the district say she is no different now than the day she was hired. There is a belief that, when appropriate, she can act charming, and apparently she did just that with the interviewing team that recommended her.

Lesson 3

Recruiters must improve the training of interviewers such they are able to detect a candidate's basic personality and behavior. This raises the issue of how interviews are conducted. Should districts require that all candidates be required to give an opening and a closing statement as a way to have them provide a window into their personality? Should interviews be more conversational and open-ended? Is the question-and-answer format ineffective in discerning personality and behavior? Should recruiters consider employing a personality assessment tool for all new hires? Would it be helpful if a district looked to private industry to learn of the systems they employ to identify basic personality? What can recruiters learn from other school systems, professional literature, or non-profits? What is clear, however, is the district's failure to discover an apparent personality disorder. The hiring of this teacher highlights the need to discern personality and behavior, both of which are easily detected with the appropriate recruiting strategies.

ANECDOTE 4

High school biology teacher. She is professionally prepared, but she is also professionally immature in that, to quote her department chair, "she says the dumbest things at the most inappropriate times." Some students refer to her as "bizarre" and "weird." She brings her personal experiences into the classroom and engages students at too personal a level. She was hired at a time when there was a shortage of science teachers, and she was not considered to be outstanding when hired. Her academic record was average, and she has performed at an average level. According to her current supervisor, who was part of the original interview team comprising several educators, what were thought to be "cute" little quirks in her personality at the time of hiring have grown into unprofessional behaviors.

Lesson 4

Interviewers must be better able to judge what constitutes unconventional behavior. It also raises the question whether group interviews have a way of "averaging" a candidate's qualities and, in so doing, miss the "extremes" that cause future problems.

ANECDOTE 5

Middle school special education teacher. She has been employed for five years and is only one year out of her probationary period. She is the least senior of the tenured nonperformers. There is little enthusiasm in her teaching. She has shared with her department head that she finds it difficult to enter the classroom and face students each day. A review of her transcript indicates she had barely enough credits to qualify for a special education certificate. She was actually trained as an early childhood teacher. She is an easy person to work with but is uninspired.

Lesson 5

Human relations hired the right person for the wrong job! It is critical to place a new staff member in a situation where she can be successful. She should not have been assigned to a position where the district "needed a body." If recruiters hire teachers with double certification, the recruiters must make certain that the teachers have sufficient credits in each subject area to be effective and not possess just enough credits to acquire a certificate in a minor subject area. Acquisition of a certificate is not sufficient evidence of qualification. This is a case where she must reassigned to an early childhood position no later than the next school year, regardless of whether a competent replacement is available.

ANECDOTE 6

Middle school social studies teacher. She came to the district from a high-performing school system. She also came with great references. Her reason for the move was that she had heard of the district's outstanding reputation. Her first years were spectacular, and she was considered principal material. Then, after literally inheriting a fortune from her family, she displayed an air of superiority over her colleagues. Their open resentment of her attitude turned her into a disagreeable department member. She has become uncooperative and often hostile toward department colleagues.

Lesson 6

She was the right person at the right time, but events beyond the control of the district turned her into an underperformer. Her problems are beyond what the district's professional development program is designed for, but she is a candidate for an employee assistance program. The district needs to identify an employee or supervisor who relates to her and with whom she works well to suggest the need for professional help. Every effort must be made to do so. The district will "rediscover" the "spectacular" teacher it first hired.

ANECDOTE 7

Middle school physical education instructor. He began his career in the district right out of college. He is a decent person with good skills. Now, in his tenth year, he is questioning if this is the career that he really desires. He is distracted and questions his future as a teacher because of limits on his future earnings. While not a disruptive element, he adds nothing to the talent pool with his poor attitude, demonstrated in part by his not having accepted a cocurricular assignment for years. He looks at some of his friends in business who are earning substantially more and is resentful that he chose teaching as a career.

Lesson 7

He may have been the right person at the time of hiring, but he is now a nonproductive member of his department. The district has a responsibility to counsel him on alternative opportunities outside of education where he will be able to improve his future earnings. This case also raises the question of how knowledgeable candidates are about their future earnings in education. Although a district may lose candidates, it should consider developing a worksheet that provides information to what future earnings will be based on, typical annual changes to the salary schedule, and the acquisition of advanced degrees.

ANECDOTE 8

Middle school counselor. The principal believes that this employee was never qualified to work as a counselor. His undergraduate and graduate transcripts speak poorly of his training. While there is no hard evidence, some colleagues believe he was a friend of the pupil personnel director and that some element of favoritism was involved in his hiring. This occurred before the district used interviewing committees and implemented other safeguards.

Lesson 8

This employee slipped through the cracks because of insider favoritism. Administrators remembered his being hired and recall quite clearly that he was an average candidate but that the director vouched for him. At the time of hiring, the district recruiting processes did not require an interviewer to reveal if he was a friend of a candidate. Because of hiring based on favoritism, the district now has another "counseling-out" situation.

ANECDOTE 9

Elementary school teachers. Three teachers are addressed in this anecdote: one in the third grade and two in the fifth grade. All have been in the district over ten years, with all of their experience in the same school. They are considered outstanding classroom teachers. According to the principal, all three have one behavior in common: a passionate dislike for all authority! They have been resistant to changes they do not personally ascribe to and have, on numerous occasions, scuttled efforts to make program changes. Any effort to discipline them has been futile since they can muster significant parent support. They have outlasted three principals, all of whom they helped drive out of the district. The current principal has worked with them the longest. The issue is that they are able to induct new teachers into their belief system in spite of the district's professional staff development program. Each has such a strong personality that breaking their team and reassigning them to three different schools runs the risk of the district then having three schools, each with a strong anti-administrator who can negatively influence other staff members. Since one of them is the union's building representative, it is viewed as futile to enlist the assistance of the teacher organization to help solve this matter.

Lesson 9

The district should consider two actions to address this issue. First, the district must implement an instrument that detects personality and behavior characteristics early in the recruiting process. It is likely, that with such a system, the district would have suspected these three teachers as being potential problems. We know from the experiences with other employees that people rarely change. Second, since there is no significant documentation that would allow the new principal to terminate the teachers at this time, it is best to leave them in place.

ANECDOTE 10

Two second-year teachers, one in the second grade and the other in the third. These two male teachers are experiencing difficulty adjusting to the demands of elementary school teaching but have been cooperative in volunteering for after-school cocurricular assignments. They had excellent student teaching experiences at two elementary districts in the region and had better-than-average grades in their undergraduate programs. Their current supervisors believe, however, that they were not prepared for the pace of work and that the districts in which they student taught placed great value on their cocurricular work; thus, their recommendations were not based primarily on classroom work. Although classified as underperformers, they have the potential to move to a higher performance level.

Lesson 10

A recruiter must take care, when examining references, to determine the activities on which the references are based. While every district needs teachers who assume additional duties, the candidates' primary references must be based on outstanding classroom work. This is less a case of a recruiter having failed to read between the lines in terms of reference checking than it is a simple case of not giving sufficient attention to their classroom performances in the sending districts. A telephone reference form must be such that it clearly distinguishes between classroom performance and other duties and responsibilities. Interview assessment forms should be heavily weighted toward classroom performance. Since both of these teachers are in their second year, the district needs to decide if there is time enough to move them to a higher level of performance.

ANECDOTE II

Three teachers in one elementary school, two in kindergarten and one in first grade, all in their third year. In all three cases, the issue is their lack of ability to deal with extremely aggressive parents. All three were strongly recommended by the sending districts. The principal has no doubt that they are good teachers, but they have not been able to handle their parent constituency. This pattern has been seen in the past where outstanding student teachers come to the district and then proceed to have interpersonal problems with staff or parents. In these three cases, the problem is with parents. Quality interpersonal skills are one of the qualities that the district seeks in teacher and administrator candidates. This quality is important in that classroom talent does not translate into being able to work effectively with parents. High-level interpersonal skills are one of our primary intelligences. A district needs to test for this intelligence in its initial recruiting of candidates. Unfortunately, most districts rely on the skill of the screening interviewer or members of the group interview team to detect this intelligence.

Lesson II

Based on what is known about the effectiveness of intensive mock interviews, a district may want to consider implementing them with potential candidates, with role-playing conducted by professional actors. A district can provide actors with scripts portraying the typical difficulties inexperienced teachers encounter with parents. While costly, role-playing is more economical than the expenditures made attempting to improve the performance of staff members who do not perform up to district standards.

ANECDOTE 12

Three elementary teachers in two schools, two in the second grade and one in the third. In each case, the teacher's underperforming rating is the result of excessive absences resulting in inadequate classroom preparation. On numerous occasions, their lesson plans have been incomplete or missing. All three were placed on intensive evaluation at the end of the second year. Now in their third year, there has been little noticeable improvement. The cause of their problems, excessive absenteeism, is troubling because if the district had closely examined their student teaching records, a similar pattern would have emerged.

Lesson 12

Once again, the district must consider revising its telephone reference form to include questions relating to a candidate's absenteeism during student teaching assignment. If a pattern exists during a candidate's training period, it is a warning that the pattern may continue once employed. A person's history usually speaks accurately to one's future work.

ANECDOTE 13

Three teachers in grades K–3, in two schools. As was the case with the previous teachers, they are not working at levels of performance that the district can accept. A review of their undergraduate work was undertaken, and the transcripts were an embarrassment. First, the courses for which they received credit are those taken by "professional" college athletes. The teachers had taken courses in badminton, lacrosse, gourmet cooking, and other totally unrelated subjects. The grades they received in core subjects were far below the acceptable standards for the district. Yet we have evidence that the quality of undergraduate courses is the best indicator of success, unlike graduate courses where credit is often given for attendance and where few grades below an A are ever given!

Lesson 13

The district must consider a revised method of computing grade point average. To use the system that colleges and universities employ may cause a recruiter to hire candidates who have lower-than-acceptable grades in core subjects and who have too few courses in core subjects. Consideration should be given to employing a grade point average that only considers core subjects. Then, the district should determine what it considers the minimum number of required credits in core subjects, irrespective of what a state certification bureau requires.

ANECDOTE 14

Middle school. This Spanish teacher is in his second year. Last year, at renewal time, there was no question of his ability and future success. It has been a different story this year. He was married during the summer, and his wife is expecting her first child. What is different this year is his frequent tardiness and his inability to meet the goals the department chair established. The informal feedback is that he is strapped for money and has been driving a tour bus on weekends that brings gamblers from Rhode Island to the Connecticut casinos. He is exhausted, but because his teacher salary is insufficient to meet family financial needs, he works as many hours as he can in his spare time driving a bus. Both his department chair and the principal believe he is an outstanding candidate with a bright future, and the district must find ways to help him cope with this problem.

Lesson 14

This is a case where an outstanding candidate was employed but then came face-to-face with the economic realities of teaching. The opinion of supervisors is that he is talented, the students respond well to him, and he has great potential. The district must consider what options it has available to assist him in eliminating his weekend work and to find a suitable alternative to increase his compensation in the district. His supervisors need to examine what is available in the way of extracurricular activities and tutoring type jobs as short-term, stopgap measures. In the meantime, the teacher needs to pursue advanced degrees to accelerate his movement on the salary scale. More important, the superintendent needs to exert more influence in the negotiating process to improve the entry level and early steps on the salary grid. The district and the profession stand to lose if outstanding teachers leave the profession for lack of a living wage.

ANECDOTE 15

Middle school, general science. This male teacher is in his second year of a four-year probationary period. There was no indication of poor performance the first year. In fact, first-year evaluations were well above average. The department chair stated that she saw the first sign of difficulty after the district brought the newest male member into the science department this fall. While there is no specific evidence, the sense of the chairperson is that until the newest member arrived, the staff member was dating another member of the department, a teacher who has been with us for several years and who is considered an outstanding faculty member. Unfortunately, for the district, the newest member apparently caught her fancy to the dismay of the staff member in question. It has only been since this new romance has blossomed that he has lost interest in his work and is in a constant state of depression.

Lesson 15

The recruiter made no mistakes in the hiring of the underperforming teacher. He and the district are the victims of circumstance. However, to lose a teacher over a broken romance would be unfortunate. The simple solution, and probably the only sensible one, is to transfer the newest male member to the other middle school. If the teacher whom he is dating requests a transfer, the district should also consider it but not with the same urgency as his. Her transfer should be at the convenience of the district, not hers. This system has three potentially outstanding teachers in a department where there is a national shortage of qualified candidates. While the district should not be placed in the role of Ann Landers, it needs to engineer a solution, long term, wherein all three continue to be employed.

ANECDOTE 16

Second middle school, special education. This teacher is in the first year of a four-year probationary period. His work has been below average from the beginning of his employment. Rarely has it been the case where a first-year teacher performs so poorly. The teacher graduated from an institution that has a good, but not necessarily outstanding, reputation for the training of its student teachers. There was every expectation that he would be successful. While poor classroom management is usually a problem for first-year teachers, in this case it is lack of management, plus poorly prepared lesson plans, inadequate preparation, and below-average delivery of individualized instruction. Complaints have come from parents, instructional aides, and students. The performance of this teacher prompted the human relations office to examine the files of all student teachers, regardless of subject taught for the last five years, who graduated from the same college as the underperforming teacher. The goal was to compare failure rates of newer teachers who attended that college. What the recruiter found was that in a five-year period, not counting the current year, the district hired twenty-seven teachers from this college. Of the twenty-seven, eight were non-renewed for poor performance. Six were trained in special education, and according to district records, all six had the same college supervisor during their student teacher experience! The same supervisor wrote their student teaching evaluations and the references that formed the basis for their being hired.

Lesson 16

Two strategies should be considered. First, records must be kept of all probationary teachers who are not offered tenured positions, including where they were trained and who wrote their evaluations and letters of reference. Second, the district should contact the college and report its findings for them to use in addressing an obvious problem it has with one instructor.

ANECDOTE 17

Second middle school, English. This teacher is in her third year of a probationary period. According to the comments made at the meeting, this is not a case of a failing teacher; rather, it is a situation where there are certain classes where the feedback from students and parents is somewhat negative. It appears that the teacher is competent in the teaching of literature but is not performing well in her writing classes. This raises the question about how careful the district was in examining her transcripts, since an analysis now indicates that she completed many literature classes and several courses in the classics but acquired only six credits in writing. Is it any wonder then that she is underperforming in her writing classes?

Lesson 17

Without additional course work in writing, this teacher will have to be assigned within a narrow range of courses. The larger issue, however, is what priority the district places on hiring teachers who are qualified to undertake assignments outside of their areas of specialty. Without a policy to govern hiring practices, the district will continue to make errors in hiring.

ANECDOTE 18

High school guidance counselor. While there have been no serious concerns with the administrative aspect of his work, issues have surfaced regarding the manner in which he relates to students. This is his second year, and a decision must be made within two months if he is to remain in the district. He displays a professional immaturity as a counselor in what he says and with the colloquial speech he employs to say it. His counselor-to-student ratio is a conservative 1:125, so he is not over-loaded. His principal reviewed his credentials and was reminded that the site visit that was scheduled two years ago to observe this young man in action during his student teaching assignment was canceled due to a snowstorm and never rescheduled. As a result, he was hired based on one interview at the department level and three telephone reference checks. This runs counter to the district's recruiting guidelines that call for a minimum of either two interviews on-site or one interview on-site and a site visit. In both cases, the telephone reference check needs to be completed.

Lesson 18

The district has multiple issues to contend with on this hire. First, he should not have been employed, since the recruiting guidelines were not followed. Second, a qualified interviewer would have observed the candidate's immaturity during the one interview that was held. Third, systems need to be put in place to guarantee that the required interview and site visit procedures are adhered to.

ANECDOTE 19

High school physical education. This teacher is in her first year and is assigned to grades nine through twelve. There are no issues with the quality of her education or student teaching assignment. Her recommendations from her first teaching assignment were excellent, but she was there only one year. She moved here because of her husband's transfer to the region. She is professional in her dealing with staff members, administration, and parents. There is a commitment on her part to be successful, and she has enrolled in graduate courses. Unfortunately, she is having a difficult time with the boys in her junior and senior classes. She is twenty-three years old, petite, attractive, and looks considerably younger than she is, and students want to interact with her as though they are peers. She is also sexually attractive. The boys in the classes are especially difficult for her to handle. She is trying her best, but it has become troublesome situation for her supervisor.

Lesson 19

This is less of a recruiting problem and more of a scheduling problem. Nevertheless, the recruiter has some responsibility to monitor her assignments to ensure that she has an opportunity to be successful. It is not unusual for a young, attractive female teacher to encounter problems with sexually active teenage boys. Nevertheless, if a district leads a new teacher to believe that there is a well-formulated induction and professional staff development program in place, then it has to live up to the commitment. Teachers fresh out of college are not yet fully trained, and the district needs to complete that training—in this case, providing strategies for coping with teenage boys.

ANECDOTE 20

High school social studies teacher number 1. This teacher was recruited through an alternative certification route. He majored in English as an undergraduate and has a master's degree in art history. He spent fifteen years working for an aircraft-manufacturing company in its publication department writing technical manuals used by engine inspectors. He lost his job when the work was outsourced to India. Shortly thereafter, he entered the alternative program and received his certification to teach social studies. The program consisted of eight weeks of course work that included a three-week student teaching assignment at a summer program in a regional vocational–technical school. He is highly thought of within the department, is cooperative and friendly, and is among the first to volunteer for additional assignments. His class load is similar to what other department members have been assigned, with the exception of one teacher who is trained in advanced placement work.

The issue is that he is deadly boring in class and lacks the enthusiasm and ability to motivate students. He is not well grounded in teaching strategies and has only a limited knowledge of how to structure a class for effective learning. He was hired based on two interviews and a telephone reference check. There was no opportunity to see him teach a demonstration class, and there was no reason to deny him a contract based on information received.

Lesson 20

The district needs to determine if candidates who receive certification through an alternative route are less prepared to teach than those who complete a four-year program with extensive student teaching experience. Does the lack of intensive student teaching experience in a typical high school setting create issues for candidates? Equally important, does such lack of experience deny a district the opportunity to determine if he is suited to teaching? Success in industry does not translate automatically to teaching. Should this experience require the district to develop additional methods to evaluate alternative certification applicants? Are the supervisors who judge these candidates during the summer of the same caliber as those who work during the regular college semester?

ANECDOTE 21

Social studies teacher number 2. This teacher is the newest member of the department. She worked in another state for several years. Unfortunately, her husband had an involuntary transfer, tantamount to a demotion, which brought her to this state late in the summer. The move necessitated her taking a position as soon as possible since her income was vital to the family's economic survival, given her husband's demotion. The only position open so late in the summer was one with her current district. The new position also entails a long commute in terms of both time and distance. Administrators in the district privately expressed some concern over the long commute but did not mention it during the recruiting process.

Up to now, the district policy does not allow interviewers to consider commuting distance a legitimate topic of conversation. Moreover, the district has many current employees who travel equally long distances and have never had a problem with either their attendance or performance. In this case, according to her department chair, the teacher has both attendance and performance issues, both of which have been well documented by the chair and principal. Additionally, she has been unwilling to accept any paid cocurricular assignments, preferring to leave school as soon as her required contract time has been completed.

Lesson 21

The district must explore what the legal ramifications are regarding entering commuting issues into the interview process. How does the district, with its present policy, answer to parents whose children are being denied an education with this teacher? Does the district allow a teacher to fail because of a long commute and, in the process, negatively affect students?

ANECDOTE 22

Science teachers. This involves a husband-and-wife team whose performances are not satisfactory. The principal is not pleased with the work of either teacher. They are assigned to positions that have been a problem for the district to fill in recent years: chemistry and physics. It is worth understanding how they came to be hired at all and then to be hired as a team. A member of the district's recruiting team attended the principals' national convention in San Antonio, where the district had a booth to provide information to prospective candidates. This husband–wife team spoke with the representative, learned about the two positions that were open in their respective fields, and then submitted applications with the representative. At the time, they were teaching in a small high school in a rural district in Montana.

The possibility of hiring a husband–wife team for two positions difficult to fill was almost too good to be true. There was an interview, but given the location of the district's booth on the convention floor and the tight schedule of the representative, it was at best cursory. That was in March, almost two years ago. The next step was a three-way conference call with them in April of that year and then two additional conference calls in early May. By the end of May, the district had not received any applications for either position from any other candidates. It turned out that the transcripts of the husband–wife team were average, hers somewhat better, but there were no other candidates with whom to compare them.

Under ordinary circumstances, the district would have rejected the husband's application, but to sign the wife the district had to offer a contract to the husband. Contracts were extended to both, and both accepted. Their work has been unacceptable from the outset. Neither has a command of the subject matter, and they have had no training in instructional methodology. According to the principal, if he had any options whatsoever, including using qualified short- or long-term substitutes, he would move to terminate the husband–wife team. The district considered reassigning other members of its staff but decided against such a move in that it would leave other classes without qualified instructors. The district had no viable option other than to live with the situation until June.

Lesson 22

This situation highlights what may be the most serious flaw in the district's recruiting program. The problem caught the district by surprise because it had never been in a situation where it had to hire with its back to the wall. Compounding the problem were the location of the candidates in Montana and the nature of the interview in San Antonio. The district needs to rethink how and under what circumstances it interviews at conventions. Second, the interviews must adhere to the same interviewing format that is employed when a candidates is being recruited in the district office. Third, there should be no exception to the guideline that requires all out-of-state teacher candidates to have a site visit conducted, regardless of location. Fourth, husband-and-wife applicants must be judged individually. A contract should not be extended to both if one does not meet the district's performance standards for new teachers.

ANECDOTE 23

Middle school English. This underperformer is in his second year and presents a more serious issue. He was hired in the district after four successful years in another high-achieving school system. There was no issue with his teaching performance. At the time of hiring, the district had questioned why he wanted to make a move at this time but was assured by both the candidate and his supervisor that it was a career move, even though the two districts have comparable salary schedules and contractual working conditions. The recruiter obviously did not ask the right questions. This twenty-seven-year-old is now having an affair with the mother of an eighth-grade student in his building but a student who is not one of his students. The student is not in his class and will not be at any time during the eighth grade. The mother is divorced and has just the one child, who is a very good student. It is known that her divorce settlement left her "well fixed" financially. The teacher is single and has no other romantic interest at the moment. There is evidence that he spends the weekends with her at her house and that they take family vacations together. Our issue is that he is so romantically distracted that his classroom teaching has suffered.

Lesson 23

The romantic liaison issue is essentially a nonissue given the marital status of each. He is not dating the mother of one of his students, so the district has no case to make there. This is simply a classroom-performance issue. However, the district recently learned that the teacher was "invited" to leave his last position because of an affair with the mother of one of his students. The mother was not divorced. The district needs to rethink the reference form and process employed to conduct background checks. Since it is reasonable to assume that no district volunteers this information, the hiring district needs to consult with its attorney to determine how specific recruiters can be in asking questions that address issues such as this.

SUMMARY

The anecdotes serve as a reminder to districts, including top-performing ones, that a recruiting policy needs to be developed to help its recruiters avoid the situations described. It is ever so easy to make mistakes when a policy is not in place or when it lacks clearly stated administrative guidelines. When a district lacks a policy and attendant guidelines, its recruiting process will undoubtedly change whenever there is turnover in the human relations department. Policy serves as bedrock that helps immeasurably in supporting and guiding future recruiters. It provides consistency and assurance.

Every district needs to raise questions about its recruiting process. What do we hope to achieve? What steps do we need to take to develop a reputation as having an outstanding recruiting process? What can we do to attract a more diverse and qualified staff? What would encourage top colleges and universities to place student teachers with us? How can we avoid challenges to our process? What steps must be taken to ward off patronage appointments made from inside or outside the system? How do we train our recruiters to resist political pressure? How do we attract candidates of all racial, religious, or ethnic backgrounds to apply here in large numbers? What can we learn from the anecdotes that will help us to make fewer mistakes in hiring? What steps are needed to create a level playing field for candidates?

The answers to these questions are to be found in the following five guiding principles, principles that have been and will remain the foundation on which an outstanding recruiting policy rests. The five principles must be those that the superintendent believes in and supports. Anything less than total commitment by the leader of a district results in a substandard recruiting program and a marginal school system.

First, as leader, you must have a policy, a set of protocols that establishes the philosophical underpinning of your recruiting program. The policy is your governing board's way of telling you that it supports your efforts to hire only the most qualified employees and that it expects your recruiting staff to behave professionally while doing so.

Second, you must be a leader of an ethical and moral institution. You need to believe in and practice fair play every day with every applicant. Everyone you supervise must work at keeping the playing field level. The system must be proactive in seeking the most qualified candidates. You must reject outside influence and pressure, and you must work with the governing board to encourage it to set high standards for you and your staff. The board's policy must protect you and your staff from political and patronage influences. You must demand the freedom of choice in selecting candidates. If someone wishes to work in your school system, he or she must be better than the average of everyone who is employed there. One must not be hired because of whom one knows but because of what one knows. While you may be interested in where a candidate has been, you need to be more concerned with where he or she is going. If a candidate is not fit to run with champions, your school system is not the place for him or her.

Third, you need to do your homework. You must train all employees involved in the recruiting process regardless of how minor a role they may play. Whether someone time-stamps an application, answers the phone, or signs the final contract of employment, each performs a valuable human service. Regardless of an employee's title, he or she is a member of your recruiting team.

Fourth, you must instruct your staff in how to follow the paper trail of candidates. You must be thorough in your background checks. Judgments need to be based on what you learn about a candidate as a result of a comprehensive background check and not on preconceived notions. You need to record the results of your background checks, and records must be open for all to see to the extent the law requires.

Fifth, and finally, you must always look back as a way of setting your future course. It is a process that allows you to see what is ahead. You can do this by having your administrators identify your underperformers and then determine why they are in your district. In some cases, you decide you could have recruited more effectively. With others, you learn of the district's recruiting shortcomings. In some cases, you could not have anticipated changing conditions and events that affected the teacher. In a few cases, you inherit the unwelcome human problems that time and circumstance lay at the feet of some of your colleagues.

Whatever the reason for the existence of underperformers in your district, the problems they present belong to you. You may delegate recruiting responsibilities, but you cannot delegate its failures! If you are willing to accept accolades for the successes of your district, you must accept its shortcomings. To the degree that you strengthen the recruiting program, you accelerate the district's achievements. As both stated and implied throughout this book, the district is only as good as its employees.

As a former superintendent, I know that there are times when we become discouraged because we believe we are making little headway in recruiting and retaining top-performing teachers and in moving under-performers to a higher level of performance. When discouragement sets in, it helps to remind ourselves of a paragraph in the recruiting pledge that reads as follows: "On my honor, I promise to place children only in the care of those who are qualified, who are appointed to their positions by virtue of a fair and open competition, and who are judged as qualified by those capable of making such judgments."

ABOUT THE AUTHOR

Herb Pandiscio was superintendent of schools in Avon, Connecticut, for twenty-five years before taking an early retirement. Shortly thereafter, he formed Herbert William Consulting, an administrative search firm specializing in identifying and hiring school superintendents, central office employees, and school administrators. He brings credibility to the many suggestions and ideas offered in this guide through his experience of having served as a teacher, coach, assistant principal, principal, assistant superintendent, and superintendent of schools. This was followed by more than twelve years as a search consultant, private job-coaching specialist, and interim superintendent in numerous districts.

Pandiscio has personally interviewed and hired hundreds of employees for public schools and nonprofit organizations. He has reviewed thousands of applications, received from aspiring administrators, experienced administrators seeking new positions, and teacher candidates. Throughout the years, he has documented the best and worst of candidates' job search efforts. During that same period, he documented the worst of recruiting strategies and efforts by school districts and governing boards.

His first guide, *Job Hunting in Education,* chronicled the successes and failures of job seekers. Candidates will find that guide helpful in securing a position in education.

Throughout *Job Hunting in Education,* reference was made to the responsibility of the school district, often referred to as hiring agents or recruiting personnel, to establish a system that provides a candidate every opportunity to compete for a position on a level playing field. As a search consultant, Pandiscio witnessed situations in which equity in hiring was not the case. Often the recruiting process was unfair, either through the ignorance of the hiring agent or through a deliberate effort to make it unfair. Some positions were filled through patronage, not merit. Insiders who had access to the fast track filled other positions. These experiences prompted Pandiscio to prepare a guide for hiring agents, primarily superintendents and governing boards, as well as those who recruit for them. These suggestions can improve the manner in which school districts recruit, and it will assist them in building a recruiting system based on a level playing field for all candidates. The product of his recent efforts is this book, *Recruiting Strategies for Public Schools.*